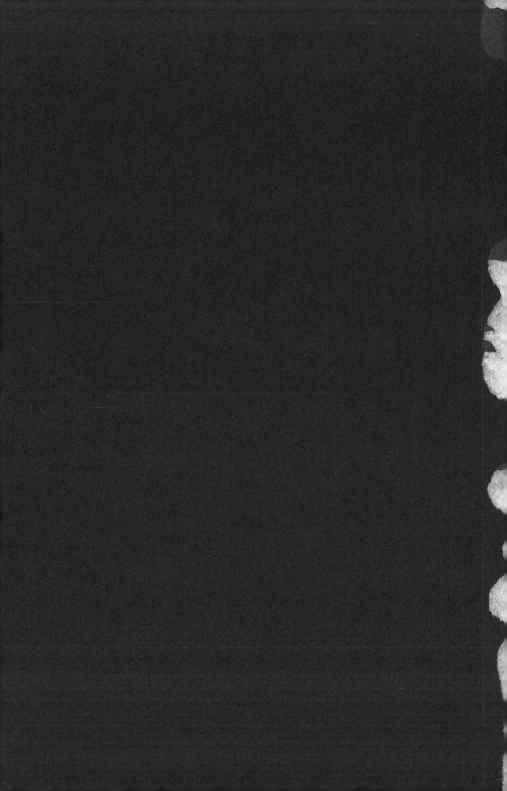

THE VILLAGE BY THE SEA

A Richard Jackson
Book

Lily and the Lost Boy

The Moonlight Man

One-Eyed Cat

A Place Apart

The Slave Dancer

Blowfish Live in the Sea

Portrait of Ivan

The Stone-Faced Boy

How Many Miles to Babylon?

THE
VILLAGE
BY THE
SEA
Paula Fox

ORCHARD BOOKS

A division of Franklin Watts, Inc.

New York

Orchard Books, 387 Park Avenue South,
New York, New York 10016

Orchard Books is a division of Franklin Watts, Inc.

Manufactured in the United States of America.
Book design by Mina Greenstein.
The text of this book is set in 12 pt. Imprint.
6   8   10   9   7

Library of Congress Cataloging-in-Publication Data
Fox, Paula. The village by the sea.
Summary: When her father enters the hospital to have open-heart
surgery, ten-year-old Emma is sent to Peconic Bay to live with her
tormented aunt and finds the experience painful until she meets a
friend who suggests making a miniature village in the sand.
[1. Aunts—Fiction. 2. Beaches—Fiction] I. Title.
PZ7.F838Vi   1988   [Fic]   88-60099
ISBN 0-531-05788-7
ISBN 0-531-08388-8 (lib. bdg.)

For Mary Fox
and again,
for Richard Jackson

Contents

THE VILLAGE BY THE SEA

1

A Question

~~~~~~~~~~~~~~~~~~~~~~~~~~~~~~~~

ᘜᘜᘜᘜᘜ

ALL that afternoon and through supper, a question
Emma wanted to ask her father stuck in her throat
like a piece of apple skin. When it was time for her
to go to bed, she felt it was her last chance. He would
be leaving for the hospital early the next morning
after Uncle Crispin came to take her to Long Island,
to Peconic Bay, where she was to stay with him and
his wife, her Aunt Bea, for two weeks.

Her father was resting in an armchair, a blanket
across his knees and an old wool scarf of her mother's
around his shoulders, even though it was the middle

of June and so warm that Emma herself was wearing a thin cotton T-shirt.

She stood close but not so close she was crowding him. He couldn't bear that now, she knew, someone leaning over him or pressing against a chair he was sitting in, even if it was her mother.

"Are you afraid?" she asked.

He touched her wrist briefly, then his hand fell back to his lap.

"I imagine there's a timid animal inside me," he said. "When it's afraid, I feel it tremble. It can't hear. It only knows the fear it feels. It doesn't have memory or an idea of the future. It lives in the present—the right now—and I try to remember it is only a part of myself, a small frightened thing I can pity. When I'm able to do that, something happens. The animal grows less afraid."

His face was nearly as white as the daisies on the table next to where Emma's mother was standing, listening. For a moment, he rested his head against the back of the chair and closed his eyes. Then he opened them and smiled at Emma.

"You know how you feel when Dr. Forde has to give you a shot?"

She nodded. But she felt that her whole self was afraid when Dr. Forde leaned toward her with the

4

hypodermic syringe in his hand. She had never imagined a scared little animal inside her that she might comfort by saying: This will be over soon. It was always her mother or her father who said that to her.

"Daddy will get better," her mother said. "The operation he's going to have has become an everyday sort of thing. Thousands of people have had heart bypass surgery."

She wanted to say: But this is my father, not thousands of people—and how can any operation be an everyday thing?

Her father was speaking in such a low voice, Emma had to lean forward to catch his words.

"I believe I will get well," he said. "One thing about being sick is that I want to tell the truth all the time. That is the truth."

He bent his head toward her as though he were about to tell her a secret. "You know that we hardly ever see Aunt Bea. We talk on the telephone at Christmas, a few holiday words. I used to call her on her birthday. It only seemed to make her angry, and she'd rake up old family troubles." He looked puzzled for a moment, then went on. "She can be a terror, but I don't think Uncle Crispin will let her make your life a misery." He laughed suddenly. "He runs her like a small-time circus. And fortunately for him, my sister is the most indolent creature in the world."

"What's indolent?" Emma asked.

"Lazy," said her mother. "She's only your half-sister, Philip," she corrected him, with a briskness in her voice that had all but disappeared these last months.

"I remember her," Emma said.

"You only saw her once," her mother noted. "And that must be at least three years ago."

"She's hard to forget," her father said faintly.

"She asked me why I was so bow-legged—"

"You're not bow-legged," her mother broke in. "That's typical of Bea."

"She had a present for me," Emma went on, recalling her aunt vividly, sitting in the very chair where her father was sitting now, how she seemed to be wearing twice as many clothes as most people wore, and how her huge gray eyes had so much white around the irises, they resembled the eyes of a big doll.

"She kept asking me why I didn't do exercises to correct my legs. I was wondering about the present she was holding. I thought she'd never give it up. I said I wasn't bow-legged, Mom, and she sort of pushed the present at me. It was a box of water-colors."

"I don't recall any present," her mother said, looking at her father, whose head had fallen back against the chair. She went to him and put her hand very gently on his neck.

"She asked me if I knew how to mix colors to make other colors," Emma said. "When I said I didn't, she said, 'ridiculous!'"

Her parents weren't listening to her. She saw how slowly her father reached up to touch her mother's hand.

Emma thought: We are all scared.

"Her laziness is a help," her father said. "She used to make fun of me when I was a kid, but she'd suddenly get bored and go off somewhere to daydream. Just stay out of her way as much as you can."

"It isn't such a long time," her mother said. "And I'll have to be away so much. You'd be stuck with babysitters."

"I'm ten," Emma said, with a touch of indignation. "I could stay alone. I have stayed alone."

"Out there on Long Island, you'll have the beach and the bay," her mother said. "Emma, I'd be worried—you here all day. And I'll be worried enough."

Emma knew there would be times when her mother might have to spend the whole day at the hospital.

Her father said, "There isn't anyone else, Emma."

He was asking her to do something for him. He was telling her how sick he was, that he didn't want her to spend one day with his sister who was nearly twenty years older than he was, and what he'd called a terror. Life was going to be hard for a while, for all of them.

She understood what he was asking of her. But she wanted to cry, to let him see tears run down her cheeks, to go to her room and slam the door, or, at least, to look gloomy and let her shoulders droop.

She saw her suitcase near the front door, and next to it, a shopping bag full of puzzles and books and a diary she hardly ever wrote in.

"What I'd like," her father began, "would be if you'd write down in your diary everything that happens—at least what is interesting or important to you. Next month, when I'm on my feet again, I'll be able to read what it was like for you out there with those two, if you'll let me. I know a diary is supposed to be private. But this time, maybe you'll keep one for both of us."

The moment for crying and looking glum had

passed. Her own heart seemed to quiver as though her father had reached out and touched it the way he had touched her mother's hand.

Her mother was giving Emma the look that stated it was past time to go to bed. She didn't want to leave them. She felt they were all in one of those places where people parted, train stations or airports.

"Why is Aunt Bea like that?" she asked, stalling.

"Envy," said her mother in a matter-of-fact way.

Her father said, "It might help if you remember that we all feel envious now and then. Haven't you?"

"Philip, she must go to bed," her mother protested. "And you don't have the strength to spare for a lecture."

"I'm not lecturing," he said, his voice momentarily strong, "I envy anyone with a healthy heart."

Emma stared at her father. The little animal of fear inside her had grown very large. Her mother came to her side and stroked her hair. "I'll telephone you every evening," she said.

"I'll call you, too," her father said, "as soon as I can."

2

Uncle Crispin

EMMA wondered if Uncle Crispin had been somewhere around the day Aunt Bea had given her the
watercolors. Aunt Bea filled the whole space of her
memory just as she had filled the chair. Still, she
thought she would have remembered him if he'd
been there, he was so tall and so thin, and his eyes
were a color she'd never seen before, yellowish, almost golden and flecked with green spots.

His head was bent forward tensely as he drove
along the twisting highways. Huge trucks passed
with explosions of wind that rattled and rocked the
little car they were in. Now and then he took one

hand from the steering wheel he was gripping so tightly and pressed a leather patch that had come partly loose from an elbow of his tweed jacket. He glanced at Emma and smiled.

"I don't suppose you have a needle and thread?" he asked. "Though if we stopped here for a bit of sewing, I daresay the authorities would cart us away. Aren't these roads dreadful? I always think I'll take the wrong ramp and never be heard from again. Or else a truck will scoop up the car and hurl it into the heavens."

"Are you from England?" Emma asked.

"Yes. I was born in St. Ives, in Cornwall. I think there's a nursery rhyme, isn't there?"

Emma hesitated a moment, then recited:

> *"As I was going to St. Ives,*
> *I met a man with seven wives.*
> *Each wife had seven sacks,*
> *Each sack had seven cats,*
> *Each cat had seven kits:*
> *Kits, cats, sacks, and wives,*
> *How many were going to St. Ives?"*

"That's the one," said Uncle Crispin. "Do you happen to know the answer?"

His voice was soft, and he spoke to her so politely she guessed he hadn't spent much time with children and hadn't heard what they were supposed to be like. She didn't shout out the answer as she would have ordinarily, but said, "One," in as polite a way as he'd spoken.

"I think so," he said. "Though there are those who say no one was going to St. Ives. Rather a sad little rhyme, isn't it? Well, when I was fourteen or so, my father and mother brought me to your country, now mine, too. I went to school and studied the violin and eventually became a teacher of music. Did you know your father was once a student of mine? Ah . . . here's the last ramp I have to worry about. Your Aunt Bea says I have as much sense of direction as a sofa. But now it's a straight road all the way."

"I think I knew you were my father's teacher," Emma said.

"That's how I met Bea," he continued. "Your father and I became friends. One day, long before he met your mother, I took him a piece of rare violin music I had come across, and there was his sister, Beatrice, who had dropped by to visit him."

Recalling Aunt Bea, how she sat in the chair as unmoving as a large stone, it was hard for Emma to imagine her dropping by anyplace. That visit had been years ago. Maybe Aunt Bea was only half a terror then. Time changed people. Emma had seen photographs of her parents when they were children. Would anyone have guessed how that thin little boy or the plump, sleepy-looking little girl would look twenty-five years later? With her own thick brown hair that she could hardly drag a comb through some mornings, and ordinary blue eyes, how would she look twenty-five years from now?

What color had Uncle Crispin's hair been before it had turned so white? He looked nearly as old as her only living grandparent, her mother's father, who lived in California and whom she had once visited for a week.

Her grandfather had a horse called Wraith, she recalled, and she had been lifted up to sit in the saddle with him. How scared and joyful she had been, high above the ground on a living animal! It made her happy now, thinking of the ride they had taken through a great wide meadow of tall grass which brushed against her bare legs, her grandfather's arm strong around her waist. The memory blew away like mist in a breeze. She was back in the present, in the worry of her father's illness, the worry of what it was going to be like living with Aunt Bea for two weeks.

14

"Your father was a gifted violinist," Uncle Crispin said. "In a way, I'm sorry he didn't go on with his career. But it's a hard life being a concert violinist—there are so many good musicians struggling to find work. I'm sure he's a fine teacher. Are you interested in music? Do you play?"

"The recorder," she replied. "Everybody in school has to learn to play."

"Good!" he said as though he really meant it. "You'll find it an immense comfort as time goes on. I teach most of the year and give private lessons in the summer. But I try to play for myself every day. A life without music would hardly be life."

The idea that music could be a comfort was a new one for Emma. When her father played his violin at home in the small room off the kitchen which was like a big closet, his forehead wrinkled, his mouth was shut tight, and he looked lost in a dream.

"Is it strange to have your father teaching in your own school? Do you have to take his class?" he asked.

"He's the only music teacher, so I have to," she answered. She hadn't thought it strange; it was certainly difficult at times. The children teased her and said her father went to sleep and snored in some of his classes. It wasn't true but she felt embarrassed just the same. Yet if she happened to pass his class-

15

room and glimpse students looking at him with interest, she felt proud.

"Teachers' kids get scholarships," she said. "That's why I go to the school." There were days when she wished she went to a school where she didn't know anyone except a few other children, where teachers didn't give her a special smile when they passed her in the corridors.

"It must be hard for you to think about anything but your father right now," Uncle Crispin said. "My mother was very sick for a time when I was a boy. I remember I felt as if I was sitting on a little chair in a huge empty house, no people, or cats or dogs, no books and furniture and pictures, and that I wouldn't be able to get up and move until she returned from hospital to give me her hand. Isn't that odd?"

"But she did come back," Emma said, her heart suddenly pounding.

"Yes, she came back," he answered. "And so will your father. I'm sure of that. I've been reading up on the operation. The doctors have it down pat these days."

She didn't want to hear about the operation right now. She asked him quickly about his name. "I never knew anyone called Crispin," she said.

"It's not too common, but you run across it every so often. St. Crispin was a Christian missionary in Gaul. He was martyred in 287. He was a shoemaker and is the patron saint of all shoemakers. When you come to read Shakespeare, his *Henry the Fifth*, you'll find Crispin there:

This story shall the good man teach his son;
And Crispin Crispian shall ne'er go by,
From this day to the ending of the world,
But we in it shall be remembered—
We few, we happy few, we band of brothers;
For he today that sheds his blood with me
Shall be my brother. . . ."

Emma was startled. He seemed for a moment to have become another person, his voice booming, one hand gesturing at the windshield. But when he spoke again, it was in the mild, slightly apologetic voice she was getting used to.

"We've exchanged rhymes," he said, smiling, "so we shall be friends."

"What does martyred mean?" asked Emma, rather hoping he wouldn't burst into poetry again.

"To die for your faith," he replied.

They had left the gasoline stations and shopping

17

malls behind them. Sparse woods of stunted pine trees grew beside the road.

"See how the sky has grown so vast," he said. "It's because we're close to the sea."

She had noticed the light changing, touching the dark green pines with a white gleam. In the bright blue sky, she saw the white spark of an airplane's wing.

"Nearly there," Uncle Crispin said after a while. A few minutes later, he turned off the blacktop onto a sand road that led through thick strands of pine and oak, many of the trees not much taller than Emma.

Uncle Crispin stopped the car.

"Emma, I want you to know how welcome you are. We're so glad to have this chance to know you— even in this circumstance." He fell silent.

Emma wondered if she should thank him. He was fiddling with the loose patch on his jacket again. His hand fell back to the steering wheel as he turned directly to her. "Your Aunt Bea is a changeable crea- ture," he said. "She's harder on herself, really, than on anyone else. But sometimes she can be a little sharp. You'll learn, though, that her bark is really much worse than her bite. And, you see, we haven't had children stay with us. She tires easily. I do hope

18

you will understand. . . ." He smiled at her, his eyes like two golden fish in his lined face. But there was worry there, too. This last year she had learned to recognize that look on the faces of grown-ups.

He peered through the windshield. "See," he said, "there's our chimney. We have lovely fires in winter when the wind blows cold off the water."

He gave a deep sigh and started the car. Had he said all he'd meant to about Aunt Bea? She was afraid, sitting in the warm sunlight that poured into the car as though it were a pitcher to be filled up. She longed to be home. There had been something hidden in Uncle Crispin's words. They don't want me here, Emma thought, and I don't want to be here either.

She imagined her mother calling them, saying, "Please take our little hippopotamus. She only weighs a thousand pounds and won't be a bit of trouble." She grinned. What would Uncle Crispin say if she told him what she was thinking? They went over a bump. "Here we are," he said.

When her father had told her Aunt Bea and Uncle Crispin lived in a log cabin, Emma had thought their house would look like the set of Lincoln Logs someone had given her for Christmas a few years ago. But as Uncle Crispin drove out from among the trees onto a large circular clearing covered with broken white shells, she saw that the house was not at all like the small cabin in the woods she had had in mind.

It was built of logs, but it was huge. In the brilliant light, it looked like a fort, dark against the sky, the shades pulled down on most of its many windows, and thick tangled shrubbery crowding up against its foundation. Two cement steps led to a broad door, the bolt across it rusty and ancient-looking.

"Your grandfather built it for his first wife, Bea's mother, in the days when such a place was called a bungalow," Uncle Crispin said. "After she died, he kept adding on rooms. Then he married your father's mother and they moved to Connecticut. He left the house to Bea in his will. It looks overwhelming, doesn't it? We use only a few of the rooms. We never use that back door. The entrance faces the bay."

They got out and walked around to the front of the house. A blaze of blue water stretched as far as Emma could see. In the far distance, small islands appeared to float above the bay, moored in their own shadows.

She ran across the hummocky grass to the railing of a wooden staircase that led down a steep cliff to a beach below. A gull swam through the air with strong strokes of its wings then drifted slowly downward like a feather, coming to rest on a post in the water.

"That post is all that's left of the dock your grandfather built for his boats," Uncle Crispin said. "Aren't gulls comical? The way they find the only roosting spot for miles around?"

Out on the water, Emma saw a white sail like an angel's wing suddenly collapse, and a small figure in the boat grabbing up armfuls of sail. "He's probably going to turn on his motor and go through that canal over there to the right," Uncle Crispin explained. "It leads to the ocean. In a month from now, there'll be so many boats trying to go through, it will look like a line waiting to go into a movie."

"Will I be able to swim?" Emma asked.

"Oh, yes . . . though the water is still quite cold. But you won't go over your depth, will you?"

"No. I'm not such a great swimmer," Emma said. "Do you and Aunt Bea swim a lot?"

"I go in but Bea doesn't care for bathing. And the stairs would be difficult for her to manage. They're fairly shaky. She doesn't like crowds. By the time the water warms up in July, there'll be dozens of people on the beach. More come every summer, and more houses are built and more shops for all the newcomers."

He didn't look as sad as he sounded. "It's no one's fault the world is getting so crowded," he said.

"Uncle Crispin—I've been wondering about the color of your eyes. What's it called?"

He laughed and touched her lightly on her shoulder. "How nice to have one's eyes noticed," he said. "I think the word is hazel. It's unusual, isn't it?"

He speaks about himself as though he were someone else, Emma thought, as though he were that gull sitting on the post or the sailor who was, she noted, now entering the canal leading to the ocean.

"Why don't you go and say hello to Bea? I'll fetch your things from the car." He waved toward the long porch that ran along the front of the house. At one end a large tangle of small pink wind-blown roses grew on a trellis. Six rocking chairs sat on the porch and scattered among them on the wide boards were several cups and saucers. As she walked slowly up the wooden steps, she saw the cups were empty but stained with tea or coffee. Behind the screen door in front of her, it was dark.

She hesitated and looked once more at the bright

bay. If only she could run down the rickety stairs to that beach! If only she could run all the way home! How could anyone related to her father be a terror? What did it mean?

She turned to the door and opened it quickly.

3

Aunt Bea

CAUTION made Emma put one foot behind her to ease the screen door so that it wouldn't bang. She found herself in an entrance room of some sort. For the moment it took her eyes to adjust to the dimness, she saw only the dull gleam of a string of keys hanging from a hook on the wall before her. She put out one hand and felt the folds of an umbrella and next to it the stiff canvas of a rain hat. On a narrow shelf lay a flashlight, several pale candle stubs, and still another empty teacup. In a room on her right a grand piano stood in front of shaded windows. Emma was reminded of a large grazing animal she had seen on a television nature program, but she'd forgotten what it was called.

She sensed movement on her left and turned at the moment a teapot held by a small, plump hand tilted in midair. She heard the steamy whisper of pouring tea. An arm covered in dark cloth descended and the teapot clanked as it hit a table where a woman sat. Her frizzy steel-colored hair was very long, caught at the nape of her neck by a thick putty-colored rubber band. Below the hem of her long black skirt, Emma glimpsed white moccasins, a de-sign of blue, red, and white beads across the toes.

Emma walked toward her. The woman didn't turn her head but picked up a spoon and stirred her tea languidly. The clink of spoon against china was the single sound in the shadowy room, its space largely taken up by an oval table and some chairs. A book-case stood against one wall, most of its shelves filled with dishes among which were piled a few books.

Emma swallowed noisily. "Hello, Aunt Bea," she said. "I'm Emma."

For a moment, the woman made no sign she had heard her. Then she put her spoon down in a finicky way and let out a bray of laughter that ended abruptly. "Who else would you be?" she asked. She turned her head toward Emma. "I see you're wearing blue denim like everyone else in the world," she remarked.

"I brought a dress and a skirt and two blouses," Emma said.

"You'll hardly need such an impressive wardrobe here," remarked her aunt. "Sand, sea, and sun, you know," she added in a tone of voice that seemed to say such things were silly.

"There wasn't much traffic," Uncle Crispin announced as he came in carrying Emma's things. He, too, had closed the screen door so quietly Emma hadn't heard it. "You'll be glad to know, Bea, that Philip was in good spirits. I think he's optimistic about the operation." He turned on a small standing light near the table.

Aunt Bea showed no sign of gladness. She had begun to scratch one hand with the fingernails of the other. She appeared entirely absorbed by what she was doing. She smoothed the hand and plucked away at her thumb, her fingers moving like small gears in an intricate machine, her head at a slight angle. She's like a parrot, Emma thought, cracking open seeds.

"One hopes he'll come through the hands of those doctors without more complications," Aunt Bea said at last, her hands at rest in her lap. "Crispin, did you remember to get my Ceylon tea?"

"Yes, I bought plenty in the city," he answered.

"One would think the idiots who run the markets out here would know enough to stock decent tea," she said. She looked into her teacup, frowned, and lifted the brown teapot again.

"Philip sent his love," said Uncle Crispin.

"His love . . ." Aunt Bea repeated thoughtfully. "What a peculiar usage. How can one *send* love?" She didn't appear to expect an answer, for she went on to speak of something entirely different. "Did you know, Emma, that the English upper classes pour milk into their cups before the tea, and the lower classes add milk after they've poured?"

There was no milk pitcher on the table. Emma didn't understand what Aunt Bea was talking about. Although she struggled to think of something to say, nothing came to her.

"It hardly makes a difference, Bea, what people do with their tea," Uncle Crispin said.

"It makes every difference," Aunt Bea said, smiling to herself as though she knew a secret that pleased her.

"I'll take Emma to her room. I'm sure she'd like to unpack and settle in," Uncle Crispin said.

Aunt Bea nodded, then asked, "What's in that shopping bag?"

"Some books," Emma replied. "Jigsaw puzzles, a diary."

She didn't mention the present at the bottom of the bag for Aunt Bea. Her mother had wrapped it hastily in newspaper at the last moment this morning, and tied it with knotted laundry string.

"Jigsaw puzzles at your age!" Aunt Bea exclaimed. "I thought only old ladies passed the time with such things. . . ."

"Well—I'm practicing," Emma said. She wished she hadn't. Had she meant to be so fresh? The words had burst out of her. But to her surprise, Aunt Bea seemed amused and emitted her braying laugh again.

"Come along, Emma," Uncle Crispin said, picking up her bag and suitcase. She followed him into a large living room crowded with furniture, most of it wicker and all of it dusty. Only the big television set looked new. In front of it was a small sofa strewn with tired-looking pillows and several articles of clothing, scarves, a sweater the color of laundry soap, and a long, soiled lilac bathrobe. On the floor, around the sofa's carved wooden feet, stood empty glasses and dirty teacups. Rusty pine boughs filled the hearth of a large stone fireplace.

"I must clean up around here," muttered Uncle Crispin.

The room was gloomy and dark like the other rooms except for a deep straw basket overflowing with knitted things, small blankets and shawls in luminous shades of mauve and rose.

They went up wide uncarpeted stairs to a hall along which were seven or eight closed doors. A narrow, tall window at the end of the hall framed the tops of pine trees and the sky.

Uncle Crispin opened one of the doors. "We thought you'd like to be able to see the bay," he said. Sunlight streamed through unshaded windows onto gray floorboards and an oval braided rug. He put her things next to a bed. On its wooden headboard was painted a large, lily-like blue flower with curling leaves; an afghan throw in shades of green lay across the foot of the bed. "Your Aunt Bea made that," Uncle Crispin said, pointing to the throw. "She's a marvel with wool. She painted the flower, too. There's a table you can use for a desk. The top drawer in the bureau sticks, but if you yank hard, it will come out. Do you need more than one chair? There are dozens more in rooms we don't use. Too many chairs for the likes of us."

One chair was enough, Emma told him.

"When you've put away your things, come down

and we'll have lunch," he said. "You must be very hungry."

"It's a nice room," Emma said. She wished he wouldn't leave her alone in it though. He seemed to guess what she was feeling. He took her hand and led her to the windows. "The water is beautiful at this time of the year," he said. "It's beginning to be a summer sea. I find it comforting though I don't know why."

From the window, Emma could see the stairs leading down the cliff, and the clumps of grass she had run across. As she stared out at the bay, she remembered the little house in northern New York state which her parents had rented for several summers until her father grew too ill to leave the city and his doctor.

He had played his violin in the mornings on the screened porch. At twilight, the three of them had taken walks along dirt roads and across meadows where grazing cows would raise their heads to stare at them curiously. There had been no soaring gulls there, no water except for a trickle in a tiny stream bed near the house.

Uncle Crispin sighed as he let go of Emma's hand.

"Comforting—like playing music?" she asked.

He laughed and said, "You will think I'm always looking for comfort."

She didn't think that but of Aunt Bea in her chair in the dining room, smiling faintly to herself.

"And then there is the comfort of lunch," Uncle Crispin said. "It'll be ready in a jiffy. The bathroom is two doors down on the right. There's a yellow towel for you on a rack."

He left her at the window. It was not the water she was seeing but her father in a narrow hospital bed, the same sunlight that was now warming her touching an iron bar at its foot. Her mother was there, too, sitting in a low chair beside him. They must be speaking together in low voices—perhaps about her so far away from them.

She began to unpack the shopping bag, putting her books, the two jigsaw puzzles—one for each week—and a big pad of newsprint drawing paper on the table. She opened the diary. There was only one entry, on May second:

Daddy is sicker, it read. *I have to go to school anyhow. He won't be there in Room 103, giving music lessons. Could he die?*

She put a small alarm clock on the table next to the bed, then unwrapped the present for Aunt Bea— she might have something disagreeable to say about the newspaper and string. The present was a bowl from Italy. Would it please Aunt Bea so that she would smile at Emma and not to herself? She went to the diary and with a pencil wrote the day's date. Under it, she wrote: *I'm here. Uncle Crispin is really nice although a little peculiar. The bay and the beach are great. Aunt Bea is*— but she couldn't think of one single word to sum up her feeling about her aunt. And she felt uneasy as though one of the doors in the silent hall had opened, and an unknown person had come creeping to her room to look over her shoulder and see what she had written.

Would it help if she changed her clothes? Put on a skirt and blouse? Would Aunt Bea welcome her then? She didn't think so. She put everything away in the bureau, avoiding the sticking drawer. Uncle Crispin's voice called faintly from below, "Lunch, Emma . . ."

Two weeks is only fourteen days, Emma told herself as she went down the stairs.

Emma was sure Aunt Bea had not moved from her chair. She saw a glass of milk and a grilled cheese sandwich on the table near the brown teapot. She handed the Italian bowl to her aunt before she sat down to eat.

"My mother got it for you," she said. "It's from Deruta, Italy."

"I know where it's from," Aunt Bea said irritably. "If there's one thing I know about, it's faience."

"How pretty," Uncle Crispin remarked. "How thoughtful of your mother. Eat your sandwich before it gets cold, Emma."

"French faience is the best, of course," Aunt Bea said, turning the bowl in her hands. "As everyone— nearly everyone—knows."

"Really, Bea, it's a lovely bowl, so bright and cheerful," Uncle Crispin said. Aunt Bea held out the bowl without looking at either of them. Uncle Crispin took it from her quickly and put it on one of the less crowded bookshelves. It was only the impression of a second, but Emma had suspected Aunt Bea had been about to drop the bowl on the floor.

"Cheerful, I suppose that is the best word for it," she was saying. "You will thank your mother for me, Emma." She picked up a fat silver pen covered in intricate scrolls and began to do a crossword puzzle in a newspaper folded on the table in front of her.

"Can't I fix you something, Bea?" Uncle Crispin asked. He sounded as though he were asking her a favor.

34

"I'll have a bite later on," she said. "What I want now is fresh hot water for my tea."

Emma sat down. She was terribly hungry. As soon as she bit into the sandwich, she felt like a noisy parade. She had meant to drink the milk in sips but she heard herself gulp. Aunt Bea didn't look her way; she was intent on the puzzle.

"How do you spell sheets?" she demanded.

Emma started to answer but caught herself in time, drowning the *s-h* in a swallow of milk. Uncle Crispin spelled out the word. "No, no," Aunt Bea protested impatiently. "I meant bed sheets not sheets of paper."

"They're spelled the same way," Uncle Crispin said. She filled in some squares. "And was Orestes Ophelia's brother?" She looked up at her husband and waved the pen at him as though she were about to throw it.

"Laertes was her brother," Uncle Crispin answered calmly as he poured hot water into the teapot.

"Well, spell it, for heaven's sake," Aunt Bea ordered him.

He spelled it very slowly.

Emma thought of two boys in her class who asked the homeroom teacher questions in the same commanding way, as though to test her knowledge. They

35

were no more embarrassed than Aunt Bea seemed to be by their own ignorance.

She dropped the silver pen on the table. "Pastime for idiots," she said. "Why do I bother. . . ."

She began to stare fixedly at something over Emma's shoulder. Emma couldn't help turning around to see what it was.

In deep shadow near the bookcase hung a large poster of a painting she hadn't noticed until then. It was of a vast cliff towering over the sea under a sky full of thin white clouds. An arm of stone that bent in the middle like a great elbow stuck out of the cliff and dropped into the water. Just beyond rose a stone tower.

"What do you think of that?" Aunt Bea asked Emma softly.

"The cliff is so high," Emma began, "that it looks—" she hesitated, then said questioningly, "alarming?"

"Good!" exclaimed Aunt Bea. Emma didn't feel praised. There was something in the way Aunt Bea had said that word that suggested she was a dunce who had said the right thing—for once.

"What else?" asked her aunt briskly. It was like a test at school.

"There's a little boat," Emma said. "I can't see

how many people are in it. It looks like a toy next to that cliff."

Aunt Bea nodded. "The silliness of human beings next to the force of nature," she said as if to herself. "Life is a laugh." She wasn't laughing. When she went on, her voice rang out as though she were on a stage. "That happens to be a reproduction of a painting by Claude Monet—*The Cliffs at Étretat*. No one can paint like that anymore. It's all a sham these days, the painters are all fakes."

"They paint differently now, Bea," said Uncle Crispin. "There are fine painters today, too." Although he had contradicted her, his voice was agreeable, friendly. Was he running her aunt like a little circus, as her father had said?

"There you go—being *reasonable, fair!*" Aunt Bea said, and she laughed loudly, looking all around the room as though many people hidden from Emma's and Uncle Crispin's view were silently laughing with her. Uncle Crispin smiled as he went into the living room. Maybe, Emma thought, his being reasonable was an old joke between them. Aunt Bea was looking at her.

"I assume you brought the watercolors I gave you," she said. "This is the place to use them."

Emma had not used the watercolors even once.

Her voice faltering, she answered, "I didn't bring them. I'm not much good in art class. I sort of like to draw, though."

On Aunt Bea's face, Emma recognized her big doll's expression, her eyes enormous and unblinking. "The child in the neighboring house along this cliff has a blazing talent," she said. "Absolutely blazing."

She couldn't think of what to say to that. But Uncle Crispin returned from the living room, his hands filled with glasses and cups, and saved her from having to answer. Aunt Bea was still staring at her as though waiting. "I'm going to take Emma for a walk on the beach," he said.

Aunt Bea opened her mouth in a noisy yawn and sank back in her chair. She heaved herself forward, poured tea, plucked for a moment at her fingers, and once more picked up the silver pen. Without a glance at the definitions, she filled in all the remaining spaces of the crossword puzzle.

Emma took her glass and plate into the kitchen. To be out of sight of her aunt, even a few feet away, was a relief. Uncle Crispin was rinsing cups in the sink. He glanced at her briefly. "You would like a walk, wouldn't you?" he asked in a low voice. She nodded. He lined up the dripping cups on the counter. "Aren't they pretty?" he commented. "So many ordinary things are pretty, so nice. You have only to look at them."

Emma looked at him, not at the cups. She felt a rush of affection for him. She didn't know if he was ordinary, but he was certainly nice.

Aunt Bea paid no attention to them as they went past her to the screen door. Once out of the house, Emma felt free for the first time since she had awakened that morning in her own bed.

She ran ahead of Uncle Crispin and, holding on to the narrow splintery handrail, went down the tottery stairs to the beach and jumped into the sand. She raced to the water which curled against the shore in waves not much larger than Emma's fists. There was so much to look at—pebbles and shells, seaweed, worn bits of glass and driftwood.

She waited for Uncle Crispin, who picked his way across the sand like a cat. "I hate sand in my shoes," he said as he joined her at the water's edge. For a while they walked along on the firmer sand. Now and then he would point out something to her: a house whose shingled roof she could see—it was so close to the cliff edge—where a girl her own age, he thought, spent the summers with her grandmother. Emma wondered if the girl was the one with the blazing talent. Then a tall run-down looking house where, he told her, two ancient sisters lived with an elderly gardener who cooked their meals and did their shopping. It was rumored they had a little roulette wheel, and every night the three of them gambled until dawn.

They sat down on a damp log that had washed up on the shore. Uncle Crispin explained that a small Coast Guard cutter flying across the water was probably on a rescue mission. "Someone has got into trouble, no doubt," he said. People often came out from the city and rented sailboats without knowing the least thing about sailing.

"Look how the water changes," he went on. "Its color tells you what time of day it is."

Emma realized the water was a deeper blue than when she had first looked at the bay. A faint rosy blush touched the distant shores of the islands on the horizon.

"I can't always come down to the beach with you," he went on. "I give private violin lessons in the summer. But you can wade in the water and play on the beach."

"When we go to the country, I go out a lot by myself," she said.

He looked at her curiously a moment. "I said play on the beach—but I don't know how children play.

I think my childhood was very serious. I can recall
reading and the rooms where I read. I suppose I
must have played, too. I never cared for sports."

Grown-ups had been telling Emma to go and play
all her life. She hadn't thought about what it meant
until this moment. You played games, of course, but
there was something else the word "play" didn't seem
to fit.

"You make up things," she said, "and part of it
is like a kind of dream. You don't know what time
it is. When you pretend you're somebody else, or
you dress up a stuffed animal in baby clothes, you're
really thinking in a way that's hard to explain."

"I remember thinking a lot," Uncle Crispin said,
"but I don't believe the adults around me suspected
it."

Emma grinned. "My math teacher told me I don't
think at all," she said.

"Math is different from what we're talking about.
Music is a special way of thinking, too. What we're
talking about is imagining."

While they spoke, Emma drew a circle in the sand
with a stick. She chose two pebbles for eyes and a
piece of dried seaweed for a mouth and placed them
inside the circle. "That's my math teacher," she said.
Uncle Crispin laughed. "A startling resemblance,

41

I'm sure," he said. "I guess we'd best go back. I hope you like roast chicken. I'm not bad at that."

They had walked a good distance from the stairs, Emma realized. She had been happy for a while. Every step that brought them closer to the big log house pressed the happiness further into the sand. It was like walking to the place where you would get bad news.

"Your Aunt Bea is a smashing cook," Uncle Crispin said. "The trouble is she puts too much effort into it and wears herself out. She won't settle for ordinary cooking. I'm sure she will do you a fine dinner before you go home. Then you'll see. . . ."

What she saw was the way Uncle Crispin's forehead wrinkled when he spoke of his wife.

They reached the stairs. Emma started up very slowly. Uncle Crispin put his hand on her shoulder. It was a light touch. But then, everything he did was light and quick. He was like a grasshopper hiding in tall grass, suddenly leaping into sight for a brief moment, she thought.

"Philip is young," he told her. "That is the great thing. Youth and strength make a great difference."

She realized she hadn't given a thought to her father for the last hour or so. How could you forget someone in trouble for even a moment if that someone was one of the two most important people in your life? Yet she had.

Perhaps she was as gross as Jay Withers, a boy in her homeroom whose glittering black eyes widened with laughter when he knocked into a kid in the school corridor and made her drop her books, or yapped at stray, frightened dogs when the class was taken to the park during a recreation period. Thinking about Jay gave her a strange kind of comfort as she looked at the porch, the dining room windows behind which sat Aunt Bea. Jay was back in the city where her home was.

4

Night Voices

𝕎𝕎𝕎𝕎𝕎

A RAY of sunlight slid under the drawn shade of a dining room window and touched the bottom of the poster of Monet's cliff with a burst of glimmering brightness. Aunt Bea must have moved during their absence, for she had changed her clothes. She was wearing a long beige linen skirt and the thick cotton sweater Emma had seen on the couch in the living room.

The skirt was wrinkled and the sweater was full of holes, but she looked what Emma was sure her mother would call dashing. It was a puzzling thought. The last thing Aunt Bea was likely to do was to dash off anywhere. She was winding a ball of wool from a skein on the table. The teapot was steaming. There must be rivers and brooks and still ponds of tea throughout Aunt Bea's body, thought Emma.

"Here's some divine blackberry jam I made last autumn," Aunt Bea said, nodding toward a glass jar. "If you want to make yourself some toast . . ."

"What a treat," Uncle Crispin said and went to the kitchen. Shortly he brought back a plate of toast. Aunt Bea wound the wool steadily, her head bent over her hands. Emma stood on the other side of the table from her, not sure whether she should pull out a chair and sit down or what she should do.

That was part of Aunt Bea's being a terror. She forced Emma to think about every single movement she made. Uncle Crispin spread a piece of toast with jam and held it out to Emma. She took it, then before she could stop herself, she asked, "Do you know the joke about where the six-hundred pound gorilla sits down?" Uncle Crispin smiled encouragingly. Aunt Bea bent further over the wool.

"Where does he sit down?" asked Uncle Crispin.

"Wherever he wants to," Emma said. She and Uncle Crispin laughed. Aunt Bea broke off the yarn and looked up unsmiling, straight at Emma.

"When young people have heart trouble, it's more serious for them than for old people," she said flatly. Emma felt as if she had been suddenly slapped hard on the back and had all the air knocked out of her.

"You ought not to say that, Bea," Uncle Crispin said, the laughter gone from his face. He looked stern and distant. Emma stole a glance at Aunt Bea. She had begun winding another ball of yarn. Her face was as blank as a sheet of paper.

"The operation is supposed to make him well," Emma said. Her voice sounded very small in the silent room.

"And it will," Uncle Crispin said firmly.

"One hopes so," murmured Aunt Bea. "Do eat your toast, Emma."

"I must put the chicken in the oven," Uncle Crispin said, going back to the kitchen.

Emma bit into the toast. The jam really was divine. She started to say so, but words of praise wouldn't come to her lips. Instead, she said she wanted to go to her room and work on a puzzle. Aunt Bea looked up at the Monet poster, her hands still. She wants me to look at it, Emma thought, and I won't. She felt thorny and sad. She finished up the toast quickly. She knew she would end up hating that poster.

Once in her room, she closed the door and went to the table where she opened the pad of newsprint. With a blue crayon, she drew a calendar for the days she was to be away from home. It filled an entire page. She had held the crayon so tightly that her hands were streaked with blue wax. She lay down on the bed and read *The Secret Garden* for a while but found she couldn't concentrate. At last she gave up trying and went down the hall to the bathroom.

Aunt Bea must have taken a bath before she'd changed her clothes. There was still steam on the medicine chest mirror. Hanging from a hook on the door were four or five bedraggled cotton bathrobes. Two damp towels lay on the floor. Dozens of small jars of creams stood on the windowsill, their lids scattered amidst them. There were balls of dust everywhere. Peering at a large one beneath the sink, she saw a flash of white at its center. She knelt and plucked it out. It was a plastic deer not longer than an inch. A string was tied through a loop between its tiny antlers. Emma looked at it curiously, then put it in her pocket. She found a yellow towel she guessed was hers bunched up in a corner near the tub.

The hall was utterly silent. She pretended for a moment that Aunt Bea and Uncle Crispin had gone away. She would be able to manage by herself—though maybe it would be spooky at night. Her mother had given her ten dollars in case she needed something. There was probably a store not far away where she could buy a few groceries. She began to love the idea, and the pleasure of it set her running down the hall to the narrow window. But the thump of her own feet on the floor broke into her dream. Uncle Crispin, she knew, would not leave her alone. She wasn't so sure about Aunt Bea.

Looking out over the tops of the pine trees, she spotted the roof of a house, the place where the girl and her grandmother spent the summer, a two- or three-minute walk through the little wood, she guessed. A phone rang from below. A moment or two later, Uncle Crispin called up from the living room, "Emma, it's for you."

The phone sat on the end of the long table next to a closed violin case. Uncle Crispin, wearing a blue canvas apron, held out the receiver to Emma. She took it eagerly, noticing at the same time how gently his other hand rested on the case. For an instant, it seemed to her he was petting it as if it were a beloved creature. "Your mother," he whispered.

"Oh, Mom!" Emma breathed.

"Daddy is settled in," her mother told her. "He

has a lovely nurse named Lucy Biggs and his window looks out on the East River."

Emma's eyes filled with tears. She could not speak.

"Emma?" Her mother's voice was alarmed. "Uncle Crispin says you've settled in, too—that you had a walk on the beach with him. . . ."

"I'm okay," Emma managed to say. She could see Aunt Bea's back, her moving elbows.

"You don't sound okay," her mother said.

Uncle Crispin had gone back to the dining room. Emma pressed the phone against her mouth. "Is it true what Aunt Bea said?" she said, almost whispering. "That when you're young, heart trouble is more serious?"

"The same old Bea," her mother said grimly. "Listen, Emma. Heart trouble is always serious. But everything is looking hopeful for your father. I want you to be hopeful, too." She was speaking slowly, trying to be patient. Emma longed for the weight of her mother's arm around her shoulders, the way she would run one finger across her forehead and around her face as though she were tracing it.

"I'll be hopeful," Emma said, wondering how you could feel hope when fear, like a thick fog, hid everything but itself. "Are you going to call me tomorrow?" she asked.

"Of course I am," her mother said. "I'm going to call you all the time." Emma pressed the receiver closer to her ear. "But Uncle Crispin—he is nice, isn't he?" her mother said. "A patient, kind person."

"Yes . . . he's cooking our supper right now," Emma answered.

"I have to go back to Daddy, Emma."

Emma thought she could actually hear the miles between them as though each one of them was a small bell, sixty-five of them all striking, the sounds growing ever fainter. Her mother was only half there on the other end of the wire; the rest of her was walking back down the hospital corridor to her father.

"When will you call?" asked Emma.

"As soon as I can," said her mother. Then the phone went silent; her mother was entirely gone.

She went to the window that looked out on the bay. The water was as red as blood in the sunset. The far islands bloomed like blood-red roses. She turned away to the dining room. Aunt Bea was playing a hand of solitaire. Her fingers tapped the back of each card before she put it down. Tap, tap, tap, her fingers clicked like fast heartbeats.

"Supper," announced Uncle Crispin. Emma went in. The table reminded her of something she'd read in a story long ago. There were balls of wool, playing cards laid out for solitaire, the brown teapot, empty cups, the newspaper with the filled-in crossword puzzle, Aunt Bea's silver pen, and three plates and flatware. She remembered. It was a bit like the Mad Hatter's tea party in *Alice in Wonderland*. Aunt Bea looked as sleepy as the dormouse but her hands were moving, touching the plate in front of her, the pen, the wool, with restless fingers.

The roast chicken and baked yams were good. Uncle Crispin told Emma about one of his students, an elderly woman whose arthritis had nearly disappeared because of the exertion of playing the violin.

"What the violin requires is talent," Aunt Bea interrupted shrilly.

"It needs physical strength, too," Uncle Crispin said. For a little while, Aunt Bea ate and was silent. Still, Emma found herself waiting as though for a loud alarm clock to ring. She wasn't as startled as she might have been, earlier in the day, when Aunt Bea exclaimed loudly and scornfully, "Canned peas!"

"At least, they're French canned peas," Uncle Crispin observed with a smile.

"At least . . ." Aunt Bea mocked. But she smiled, too.

When the saucers of chocolate ice cream were set down on the table, Aunt Bea looked at Emma. "Have you seen the Connecticut estate?" she asked.

Emma looked at her blankly.

"The house my father built for your grandmother?" she asked more loudly, as though Emma were deaf.

Emma shook her head. "They both died before I was born," she said.

"Well, of course, I knew that," Aunt Bea declared. "You're grandmother *made* him build that place— using my poor, dead mother's wealth. Everybody knew that! I admit it was a beautiful house. My father had style and your grandmother had push. I was at Smith College then. They never invited me— not once—to visit there."

"That isn't quite true, Bea," Uncle Crispin reproached her. "You've often told me about spending Christmases there."

"Those are fairy tales," Aunt Bea said self-righteously. "I was just a lonely girl. Can you blame me for making up stories? It's too pathetic! I thought Philip might have taken you, Emma, to see the place where he grew up. God knows what sort of people own it now. I'm sure it's worth a fortune." She swallowed a spoonful of ice cream and scraped the saucer fiercely. "All I inherited was this nightmare of a cabin."

"This is a fine house," Uncle Crispin disagreed. "We're lucky to have it, and the bay and the countryside are splendid."

"It's a nightmare," Aunt Bea said insistently, "and the countryside is nothing but a tired suburb."

Emma helped to clear the table. Aunt Bea grabbed up her cards and spread them out in another hand of solitaire, slapping the table with them.

In the kitchen, Uncle Crispin washed and Emma dried. She heard the scrape of chair legs against the floor. A moment later, television voices murmured from the living room.

Emma had never heard of any Connecticut estate. Those grandparents had always seemed far away from her, buried in time, like people she might read about in a history book. The way Aunt Bea had spoken made her feel she was to blame for some mysterious trouble that had occurred years before she was born.

"You're a helpful girl," commented Uncle Crispin.

She wanted to ask him about that trouble. Aunt Bea had been smoldering so, banging her plate, slapping down the cards. "I don't think Mom and Daddy have a lot of money," she said. "I never heard about the estate."

Uncle Crispin sighed. "It's all ancient history," he said. "I think the place was sold for taxes years ago. I know your father had to work hard to stay in music school. I'm afraid your Aunt Bea broods about the past too much."

Emma leaned against the counter, watching him scour out the sink. She felt a hard lump in he jeans' pocket. She reached in and took out the plastic deer.

"Look what I found in the bathroom," she said, holding it up to him. "It's only plastic but it's pretty, isn't it?"

Uncle Crispin dropped the sponge he had been using and snatched the deer from her hand to look at it closely.

"Where was it?" he demanded. He stared at the deer as though it were a biting insect.

"Under the sink, in a dust ball," she answered uneasily.

He dropped it in his shirt pocket. Without another word, he put away the scouring powder and sponge.

Emma went to the living room and stood uncertainly for a moment next to the fireplace.

Aunt Bea patted a cushion on the little sofa. "Come sit with me and watch this movie," she said, smiling at Emma. "It's a good one. I've seen it three times. You see that little boy? You can tell he's lower class by his cheap suit. Look at that ridiculous suit! But he's *adorable*, isn't he? And he's going to get into all kinds of trouble, carrying messages between that man and woman who are in love."

Emma, astonished by this outburst, sat down. Aunt Bea suddenly put her arm around her and giggled. "We'll be all cozy here and watch together, shall we? Now . . . ssh!"

Uncle Crispin came into the room and went to the long table where he sat down and began to look through a sheaf of music. He sat stiffly as though he were balancing an object on his head. When Aunt Bea withdrew her arm, Emma was relieved. It had begun to feel like a log on her back.

"Don't you want to see the wonderful English countryside in the movie, Crispin?" Aunt Bea called out gaily.

"I have seen it," Uncle Crispin replied curtly.

Emma glanced at her aunt, who had made a little moaning sound like a puppy. She was staring at her husband's stiff back, looking as baffled as Emma felt. She doesn't get her way all the time, Emma thought to herself.

She turned her attention to the movie. The little boy who carried messages for the man and woman who loved each other didn't understand what was going on between them, any more than Emma understood why Uncle Crispin had grown so distant since he had taken the deer from her hands, or why Aunt Bea was acting so fondly toward her.

"Don't you hate commercial ads?" Aunt Bea asked during a break in the movie. "Everybody seems so stupid—talking in those horribly cheery voices!"

Emma hadn't given much thought to the people who tried to sell you things during commercials. You waited until they were over. But her aunt's friendliness encouraged her to ask a question. "You said there was a girl next door? The one who's so good at watercolors? Is she here yet?"

"Oh—that girl. The grandmother is an old busybody; she used to drop in, uninvited, but I put a stop to that. What is that girl's name, Crispin? Ontario? Quebec?"

"Alberta," stated Uncle Crispin, not turning around.

"Why, yes," said Aunt Bea. "Imagine naming a

child after a Canadian province! She'll be someone for you to play with. Of course, some children play wonderfully by themselves. I always did. But then I was imaginative." She gave Emma a sunny smile as though she'd complimented her.

Two weeks isn't long enough to get used to such a person, Emma thought.

"I think I'll go to bed now," Emma said.

"But the movie isn't nearly over—don't you want to watch it with me?" Aunt Bea asked her plaintively.

"I'm pretty tired," Emma said. She was never too tired at home to stay up on those special occasions when Daddy would say, Oh, let her stay up just this time, even when she could hardly keep her eyes open.

"Tired!" exclaimed Aunt Bea. "A young girl like you! How truly boring!" She turned from Emma and leaned forward intently, her eyes on the television screen.

"Of course you must be tired, Emma," Uncle Crispin said. His voice was gentle and light again, not the way it had been in the kitchen when he questioned her about the deer. Emma looked at her aunt. "Good night," she said softly. There was no reply.

At the foot of the stairs, Uncle Crispin asked, "Do

you think you have enough blankets? It can be quite chilly even at this time of year."

"I don't need any more," Emma answered, wanting only to be alone in her room.

"Good night, my dear," he said.

As soon as Emma closed her door, she turned on the small lamp on the bedside table and went quickly to the calendar she had drawn. She took a red crayon and drew a thick X in the first box. The first day was over.

SHE woke up and for a moment had no idea of where she was. The full yellow moon looked pasted to the pane like a little kid's drawing on a school window. She heard voices. For a while she lay there listening to the distant sounds of them. They grew louder. Emma got up and opened her door a crack.

"I didn't," Aunt Bea was saying over and over again.

"Where did you hide the brandy bottle?" Uncle Crispin cried. "Where did you hide it, Bea! Don't you think I know where that plastic deer comes from? Didn't I find those deer all over the house where you used to drop them on the floor after you'd yanked them from the bottles?"

"It's an old one." Aunt Bea's voice rose to a wail. "I swear it. You know I've stopped drinking, Crispin."

"Have you, Bea? Have you? I want to believe it."

"You know how I save everything," her aunt went on in a calmer way. "You know I've stopped all that."

There was a long pause. Then Uncle Crispin said, "I do want to believe that. But you act as if you're still drinking. As if in your mind—all right, then, now hush."

"If you don't believe me, who will?" Aunt Bea asked sadly.

Their voices dropped to a murmur. Then there was utter silence. Emma crept back into her bed, pulling the cover over her head. "Daddy," she whispered into the dark.

5

The Lonely
Beach

$\mathbf{\Psi\Psi\Psi\Psi}$

"I CAN offer you coffee, plover eggs, and marmalade," Uncle Crispin said. "I also have in my larder whistling cereals, bacon with nitrates which are not supposed to be good for you, hens' eggs, and cheese. Perhaps you'd like an orange and an omelet?"

"Could I have a glass of milk and bread and butter?" Emma asked.

"Of course. I don't really have plover eggs. I was thinking about English breakfasts this morning. They start you off into the day like an overloaded donkey. Which reminds me—" he paused to pour a glass of milk and set it before her on the table— "of the time years ago Bea and I started out on a picnic. Bea and I in a very small rowboat—all that was left of her father's fleet of boats—with several lobsters, a huge picnic hamper, blankets and so forth. We were going to one of those little islands in the bay. We hadn't gone thirty feet from shore when the rowboat began to sink, and the lobsters floated out of the sack they were in and swam away."

He buttered a slice of bread, held up a jar of lemon marmalade and looked at her questioningly. She shook her head, no, wondering if Aunt Bea permitted the blackberry jam to be eaten only in her presence.

The worried expression on Uncle Crispin's face didn't match the cheer in his voice. Was he thinking about a hidden bottle of brandy? Had he thrown away the plastic deer? His voice often had a pattering effect like a light rain falling on a roof. Sometimes the patter made Emma restless.

"Now and then your Aunt Bea keeps to her room in the morning," he said, not looking at Emma. "She doesn't always sleep well."

Emma had seen people who were drunk on the streets, and once at home. A neighbor in her apartment house had come weeping to the door. He'd lost his key, he mumbled. Her father had supported him with one arm and found the key in a pocket of the man's jacket. Aunt Bea wasn't like the weeping man or the staggering people on the street. But there was something lopsided about her as though she'd lost her balance a long time ago and couldn't get it back. Emma wished she hadn't found the deer. It had been in her mind when she awoke that morning. It was quiet in her room. She heard a gull cry. She had thought of her father who, by that time, must be in an operating room.

A bypass was a little road off a main one. As she visualized such a road, it changed into a country lane she and her father and mother had walked along one early evening in upstate New York. She could see herself on the lane, carrying a musty bird's nest her father had just plucked from a bramble bush and handed to her.

A main road to her father's heart was blocked. Now there would be a lane, a bypass. She shivered and got up and quickly dressed. She had paused at the foot of the staircase, drawn a deep breath and braced herself for greeting Aunt Bea. When she discovered only Uncle Crispin in the dining room, she realized by the relief she felt how much she had dreaded seeing her aunt.

"Please, what time is it?" she asked him now. She

could hear bacon frying and see Uncle Crispin's back as he bent over the stove.

"Eight-forty exactly," he replied.

Emma looked down at the bread and butter on her plate. To take one bite of it would be like swallowing a whole loaf.

Uncle Crispin was suddenly beside her, pulling a chair close to hers and sitting down. He took a table knife and cut the bread into little pieces.

"Try eating it that way," he said in a kindly voice. The worry on his face was gone; it showed only concern for her.

"Mom's going to telephone me," Emma said breathlessly.

"She certainly will," he said. "The operation is not likely to take very long. You can go down to the beach after you eat. I'll call you the second the telephone rings."

She didn't think she could do that—leave the house before she had heard her mother's voice.

They both looked up at a shuffling noise in the living room. Aunt Bea appeared on the dining room threshold. Her hair stood up all over her head like milkweed in a wind. She was wearing one of the cotton robes Emma had seen in the bathroom. It was printed with tiny faded pink rabbits. Her feet were bare.

"Crispin. One would like the room to be darker. Can you draw the shades?"

"Good morning, Aunt Bea," Emma said.

"Tea," Aunt Bea said.

Perhaps Aunt Bea is drunk on tea, Emma thought. As she slumped into a chair, Emma realized she had just seen her aunt standing up for the first time. She was much taller than she would have guessed. It wasn't that she looked small when she was sitting down—it was that she seemed so shapeless. Uncle Crispin had drawn the shades and set the kettle to boil on the stove. Aunt Bea's eyes were closed; her hands clutched the robe, but one finger tapped against her ribcage as though something about her always had to be moving.

Recalling the voices in the middle of the night, Aunt Bea's awful wail, Uncle Crispin's angry protests, Emma looked for a sign of what had happened.

She ate two bits of bread. Uncle Crispin poured hot water into the teapot and sat down to eat his bacon.

"How cheerfully you poison yourself!" Aunt Bea exclaimed, her huge eyes open now and staring at her husband. Uncle Crispin didn't look up. He said nothing, but he certainly didn't look cheerful. Perhaps his silence was the sign, Emma thought.

"I'll go upstairs and make my bed," Emma said.

"I should think so," remarked Aunt Bea. "It's the maid's decade off. Who else would make it?"

"Bea!" protested Uncle Crispin.

Aunt Bea's fingers tightened on her robe.

"I'm sure Emma doesn't expect anyone to make her bed," he said smoothly.

Aunt Bea had been sitting rigidly, her head held high as though she were posing for a photograph. Now she sank down into her chair, looking at Emma through half-closed eyes. "Oh . . . I don't care! What do I care about bed-making. . . ." She giggled suddenly. "Poor Crispin. You're the only one who worries about such things in this house. *We* don't—do we Emma?"

Being near Aunt Bea was like being surrounded by a cloud of gnats. She was smiling and Emma could see the glint of her chalk-white, rather long teeth. Slowly, she pointed a finger at Emma, reaching out as though to poke her.

"A watched phone never rings," she said.

"I think I'll go read," Emma said.

66

"Don't tell me you're one of those children who reads all the time!" shrieked her aunt.

"Bea! What on earth are you saying!" cried Uncle Crispin.

"I say what I think—unlike other people," Aunt Bea said sulkily, and grabbed up her cup of tea.

Emma escaped into the living room. It was better yesterday when Uncle Crispin had been hearty and cheerful with her aunt—even though he had sounded a little fake.

She walked to the long table and touched the violin case. She wanted to look inside it. It might be one like her father's. He had taught her to name all the parts of a violin before she could read.

"Here. Let me show you," Uncle Crispin said, opening the cover. He had come so silently to her side, she hadn't heard his footsteps. Maybe he, too, wanted to get away from the dining room.

"It looks just like Daddy's," she said. The instrument was as beautiful as a bird in flight. When her father played, the hair-thin strings of the bow often broke. He would replace them, completely absorbed in what he was doing, his fingers so quick and practiced as he tightened a peg screw.

"Purfling," she said as she touched the border.

"That's right. Clever girl," Uncle Crispin said, and picking up the violin and placing it under his chin, he played a cadenza.

There was a loud groan from the dining room.

Uncle Crispin's face went blank. He replaced the violin in its worn blue velvet bed. "Come out on the porch," he said. "The day will lift your spirit."

He pushed aside a tattered beige curtain revealing a narrow door she hadn't known was there. It would be a way of getting out without having to go through the dining room, she thought, a way of avoiding Aunt Bea.

A cool wind, scented with pine and roses, touched her skin. "If you read out here, you will be able to hear the telephone yourself," Uncle Crispin said. "It was thoughtless of me to suggest you go to the beach."

Uncle Crispin was making her feel uneasy, too. "It's okay," she said as she usually did when she didn't understand what some grown-up person was saying to her.

"No one ever uses these sweet old rocking chairs," he said. "It's a pity."

Aunt Bea is already off her rocker, Emma thought to herself.

"I'll read here," she said to Uncle Crispin. Her

spirit might lift just a little if she could be alone for a while. He was looking at her worriedly. It was hard to reassure grown-ups when you weren't certain yourself what you were feeling and thinking—when thoughts dissolved before you could name them.

"I'm fine," she said. "Really."

"Crispin!" Aunt Bea called from the dining room. He gave Emma a quick smile and went back into the house.

She sat down for a moment in one of the chairs, imagining all six of them filled with identical Aunt Beas, rocking away the long day, cackling about the horribleness of everybody in the world except themselves and that painter, Monet, until they tipped their chairs right off the edge of the porch.

She jumped up and ran down the steps. There wasn't a book in the world that would interest her this morning.

Her father would be sleeping now—the false sleep of hospital operating rooms which she remembered from the time her tonsils were taken out. It had been like sinking into something soft and furry and thick and damp.

White clouds tumbled across the blue dome of the sky as though the wind were a great broom sweeping them all west forever. The water of the bay curled, broke into whitecaps. The islands were so distinct, Emma could see a line of yellow beach around each one of them. Down the rickety stairs was another beach, shadowed by the cliff at this hour of the morning. She leaned outward, holding to the stair post which was warm and splintery in her hand. She couldn't see a living thing below, not even a shorebird scissoring along the water's edge.

Yesterday morning her father had given her a small paperback guide to seashore life, and she had looked through it while she was waiting for Uncle Crispin to pick her up. She knew the beach was not empty, that it was teeming with tiny living creatures, some as soft as custard, others hard as stone, hidden in shells and sand and seaweed.

Yesterday morning! It seemed a week ago.

How lonely it looked down there! She imagined herself standing motionless on the sand, alone. She imagined a ring of stones around her feet, and each stone an hour that had to be spent before she walked through her own front door. "Oh!" she cried out softly, and turned back to the house.

She could hear voices from the television set. The roses on the trellis seemed to flow in the wind as though they rode a calm tide. Beneath the overhang of the porch, a small rabbit stood, its nose twitching, its paws held up. She felt terribly sleepy as if it were past midnight—a midnight with a brilliant sun burning in the dark. She sat on the grass, then lay down, and sleep broke over her like a wave.

~~~~~~~~~~~~~~~~

"EMMA, Emma. Wake up. Your mother is on the phone." It was Uncle Crispin, shaking her shoulder, calling her name.

She rose and took the steps two at a time. As she raced to the phone, she saw Aunt Bea, leaning forward, smiling, toward the television set. She heard Uncle Crispin say, "Turn it off, Bea!"

Emma pressed the receiver against her cheek.

"Emma, dear. Daddy is in the recovery room. He's still pretty knocked out. I can talk only a minute— I want to be there when he comes out of the anesthesia. The operation went well. All the news is good."

"When will he wake up?" Emma asked.

"Oh—very soon. Then he goes to a special place called Intensive Care. And if everything goes right, he can come home in a week."

"Oh, Mom . . ." Emma said.

"I know, Em. I know how you feel," her mother said. "But I must go. I'll call tonight." Then she

71

was gone. Emma put the phone down and turned. Her uncle and aunt were staring at her.

"He's all right," she said. Her heart was thumping loudly the way it did when she was frightened. Aunt Bea leaned forward and turned up the volume on the television.

"It's the best news in the world," Uncle Crispin said.

Aunt Bea looked back at Emma. "He'll like staying in bed for a while," she said. "My brother is very lazy."

"Oh, Bea . . ." muttered Uncle Crispin.

"He isn't," cried Emma.

Aunt Bea began to work on her fingers, grinning to herself. "Oh yes he is!" she said. "I know him better than you do."

An announcer's voice sounded very loud in the living room as he said, "We will now return to the hearings."

Aunt Bea stopped scratching her fingers. Her grin had broadened. She was staring at the set as though it were a delicious meal set before her. She looked up at Emma briefly. "Well, it's a good thing the doctors did something right for a change."

That was the most she was going to say, Emma felt sure. Uncle Crispin was speaking to her in a low voice, though he needn't have bothered, for Aunt Bea's rapt attention was bent on a man in a soldier's uniform whose face filled the screen. "She does care about your father," he was saying. "But you know that people express their feelings in different ways."

She could have told me she was glad, Emma thought to herself. Maybe she *wasn't* glad. Maybe she didn't know how to be glad for another person's good fortune or sad for their troubles.

"I think I'll take a walk," Emma said.

"Good!" said Uncle Crispin. "I'll make lunch and call you when it's ready."

"I'm trying to listen to these important hearings," Aunt Bea said irritably. "Give me a break!"

"Where do you get those awful expressions, Bea?" Uncle Crispin snapped.

Emma went out to the porch. The day was hers now. She walked into a small pine grove where the scent of resin pricked her nostrils. She leaned against a tree trunk, its scratchy bark against her forehead. Suddenly, to her surprise, she felt tears on her cheeks. She cried a few minutes, her arms around the tree as though it were a beloved person, thinking how odd it was that all those tears had been there inside of her, stored up like rain in a barrel.

6

Bertie

AFTER lunch, Uncle Crispin suggested they cele-
brate the happy outcome of the operation with a trip
to Montauk.

"You'd like that, Emma, wouldn't you?" he asked
her.

What would happen if the three of them were
cooped up in a car together? wondered Emma. It
was hard enough in this big house.

"How far is it?" asked Aunt Bea without enthu-
siasm. She was sitting at the dining room table,
which was strewn with sheets of cream-colored writ-

ing paper, envelopes of various sizes, the silver pen and, of course, the teapot and a cup and saucer.

"You know how far it is, Bea," he said patiently. "We've made that drive often enough."

"I have letters to write today," Aunt Bea declared.

"You could write them when we return," replied Uncle Crispin.

"Oh, yes!" cried Aunt Bea indignantly. "After you get lost, and after we spend hours in traffic jams because of all the greedy summer people who come out here in herds only to shop in those new stores that have ruined our villages. And besides, I'll miss the afternoon hearings."

"I thought you'd like to get out of the house for a bit," Uncle Crispin said. "You haven't been anywhere for days and days."

There wasn't any patience in his voice now.

"I have friends who are dying to hear from me," Aunt Bea said sulkily.

"I'm sure they can wait a few more hours," he said.

Aunt Bea looked at him suspiciously. "I hope you're not being sarcastic, Crispin," she said.

It was so hard for Emma to write letters. I did this—I did that. But Aunt Bea didn't do anything. She could write: I had eighty cups of tea today. A dreadful young person has come to stay with us, and Crispin must cook and slave for her. What kind of friends would she have? Would she write them at the same time she was watching television?

"Bea—do make an effort! I'm sure Emma would like a little distraction after what she's been through waiting to hear about Philip."

"She hasn't been through anything—yet," Aunt Bea said ominously.

They weren't looking at Emma. She knew they weren't thinking about her either. Whatever it was that was going on was between them.

Aunt Bea sighed hugely and heaved herself out of the chair. It seemed to take a long time before she was on her feet.

"For heaven's sakes!" she exclaimed. "Let's go then! I don't want to stand here forever!"

In the car, Emma stared at Uncle Crispin's white hair. He was inclined forward, and, she could see in the rearview mirror, he was squinting against the sunlight. His face was strained; he looked as though the drive they were to take was a difficult chore. Emma would have been just as glad not to have come. She had hoped the trip to Montauk would help her not think about her father. But she seemed to be thinking about him more every minute.

Hospital corridors were silent. Emma remembered that, and the hard narrow bed she had lain upon, holding her mother's hand, as the bed moved along on rubber wheels pushed by an attendant she couldn't see. Nurses had passed them carrying paper cups of medicine or little trays with something worse, a needle for one of the patients behind the half-open doors.

Her father moved so lightly on his feet. He would be lying still now in a bed with iron bars around it, a grown-up's crib.

"Look at that," Aunt Bea said from the front seat. "Isn't that new, Crispin? The trailer camp? Why do people want to live in such hideous things? I suppose a trailer has its convenience. You turn off the ignition and you're home. And look at that fat tub in a guard's uniform at the gate!" She laughed loudly. "Don't tell me they're afraid of a crime wave in there! What do they have that's worth stealing?"

"Trailers don't cost as much as houses," said Uncle Crispin. "A lot of people can't afford the kind of homes you'd approve of, Bea."

"Boo-hoo . . ." said Aunt Bea.

She was wearing a large pink straw hat that hid

her hair. Now and then she touched the brim of it with her fingers. Red and scored with scratching, her hands looked as though she'd plunged them into a thorny thicket. Emma tried not to look at them. Yet the upward movement of her aunt's arm, her wounded fingers slipping across the rosy pink straw, stirred a reluctant pity in her.

In these last months, her mother, too, had begun to do something strange to herself. Often, when she was reading a book or cooking a meal, Emma had seen her suddenly grip her arms and press them fiercely across her chest as though the apartment air had grown bitterly cold. She had known her mother's thought at those moments had been about her father's sickness.

What was Aunt Bea's thought when she tore at the flesh of her fingers?

Emma stared out the car window. She didn't want to think her mother and her aunt were alike in any way. She didn't want to feel sorry for Aunt Bea at all.

The road they were following cut through immense furrowed fields. "Potato farms," Uncle Crispin said, glancing back at Emma. At the edge of the fields, as though dropped in clumps from the sky, stood empty-looking new houses with large, shadeless windows. There was a pearly glow at the horizon as though the sea sent its own light up into the sky. Every few miles, ramps led off the road to shopping malls filled with cars.

"Stop!" Aunt Bea shrieked. "I want to go in there!"

There, Emma saw, was a tumbled-down little farmhouse at the edge of a graveled apron with a sign over the door that read: *Nice Things*.

"You won't be long, will you?" asked Uncle Crispin as he parked.

"One minute," Aunt Bea said. "Perhaps two." She scrambled out of the car, and picking up her long black cotton skirt, ran to the door and disappeared inside. It was the first time Emma had seen her move fast.

"It's the kind of thrift shop she likes," Uncle Crispin explained. "She doesn't get out of the house often. But I'll fetch her in a few moments." He sounded apologetic.

Emma sank back in the seat. It was so hot in the back of the car; she felt sleepy and jumpy at the same time. Since the phone call from her mother, her worry about her father had lessened. But she had to think about the time ahead until she could go home. She longed to be by herself.

"She has lucky hands," Uncle Crispin was saying. "She always manages to find lovely things in piles of absolute junk."

How could Uncle Crispin think Aunt Bea's hands were lucky? Emma made no comment. They sat for what seemed an hour without speaking. Another car drove onto the gravel. An elderly woman got out of it and walked to the thrift shop. The younger woman in the car held a laughing baby, lifting it up so its round head nearly touched the car roof, and then bringing it back to her lap. Aunt Bea appeared at last carrying two stuffed pillowcases, her expression triumphant. She opened the back door. "Move over," she ordered Emma roughly as she heaved the cases onto the back seat.

"You found some nice things in *Nice Things?*" asked Uncle Crispin.

"Tons!" she said. "Three perfectly good cotton bathrobes and real cotton sheets for a dollar each. Just tons! Look!" She pulled out a sheet on which Emma saw a pale gray smudge as though the person who had once used it had left a part of his shadow behind. "Just wonderful!" Aunt Bea congratulated herself.

The baby let out a shriek of laughter.

Aunt Bea was settling herself into her seat. She

glanced over at the other car. She started to giggle. "Look at that baby! Did you ever see anything so wizened? It looks a hundred years old!"

"It's a perfectly nice baby," Uncle Crispin said. "Really, Bea. How can you make fun—"

"Oh, Crispin, never mind! I have to go home. I've got a pain in my side. I shouldn't have carried that load of stuff. You might have helped me!"

"Bea, don't do this," he said.

"I'm not doing anything! I really don't feel well. I'll tell you what I will do though. We'll stop at the market—I'll pick up some food and I'll make us a divine little supper."

Uncle Crispin gripped the steering wheel as though he were drowning and it was a life saver.

"Please, Crispin," Aunt Bea said. "You know how I hate long drives. You knew that all along. You shouldn't have insisted that I come. Am I right?"

Uncle Crispin sighed. Aunt Bea turned around in her seat to gaze at the pillowcases. She smiled vaguely. Without removing her gaze from her purchases, she said, "Emma, you and Crispin simply must go to Montauk some other time. You'll love the old lighthouse."

It occurred to Emma at that moment that half the time, Aunt Bea didn't know what she was saying.

"You are the limit," Uncle Crispin said. But he turned the car around and they headed back the way they had come. Emma wasn't sorry.

Inside the joy she had felt at the news that her father had come through the operation was a sorrowful awareness that he might not have.

It was almost funny that Uncle Crispin's celebration had ended up with her crowded into a corner of the back seat next to the bulging pillowcases. Aunt Bea was humming loudly, tunelessly. Her shopping must have made her happy.

Just before Uncle Crispin drew up in front of a supermarket, Aunt Bea startled Emma by turning to her and saying, "I expect you're feeling let down. Oh, I don't mean this silly drive—though I must say, it turned out nicely for me—I mean, knowing the operation is over . . . the waiting . . ."

Her voice wasn't especially friendly. But she smiled and said, "You'll get over that, too. Everything passes. . . ." And clutching her great pink hat, she got out of the car and went into the store.

~~~~~~~~~~~~~~~~~~

IT had been a very good supper. Even though Aunt Bea—who had somehow gotten bits of parsley in her hair—giggled and boasted as she explained how she had cooked the meal, Emma liked all of it. Her aunt wanted praise for everything, she had thought, for her cooking, her cream-colored stationery, her silver pen, especially her Monet poster. Praise, praise, until stuffed with it, she toppled over into sleep, or into the sofa in front of the television set.

Now, finally, Emma was alone at the top of the cliff stairway, the guide to seashore life in her hand. There might be another hour of light, though the bay was already streaked with a reddish glow from the westering sun. A delicate breeze lifted her hair from her neck. She went slowly down, stopping to touch the blades of tall, bright green grass that grew through the cracks of the weathered steps.

At the foot of the steps, a long curling strand of black seaweed lay upon the sand like a thick snake. Along the edge of the water, its head cocked as though it listened to the soft shifting of pebbles moved back and forth by the tide, a shorebird ran on thin legs. Emma sank to her knees and leaned toward it. At once, it lifted into the air and circled out over the bay. Where light did not touch it, the water was the color of dark metal.

Tonight she would cross off another day on the calendar she had drawn. Twelve days left. It didn't sound nearly as bad as two weeks. She got up shivering a little—she could feel the night gathering itself around her, flowing from the dark green pines above, the darkening water, the sooty eastern sky—and wandered down the beach, picking up shells and small stones. When she had all she could carry, she sat down and opened the book. From the pile of shells, she chose one that resembled a tiny ram's horn, and found an illustration of it at once. It was a *limacina*.

It pleased her to find a name and a drawing of something she had picked up without thought. Did everything in the world have a name? Or were there things that were still secrets, waiting to be revealed by words?

Also in the pile were an angel's wing, a razor clam, a pale yellow lamp shell, nearly transparent, and a large winkle that for some reason reminded her of Aunt Bea's pink straw hat.

"Hey!" said a voice nearby.

She looked up. A tall, slender girl, a year or so older than she was, she guessed, stood in front of her. She was wearing tan shorts and a blue sweatshirt. Her braided hair was the color of butter. She was smiling broadly. A ray from the setting sun touched her left ear. It was like a little flame at the side of her head.

"Hello," Emma said, getting to her feet.

"You here for the summer?" asked the girl.

"For twelve more days exactly," Emma answered. "Up there." She gestured toward the stairs that led to the log house.

"Oh-ho!" the girl exclaimed. "So you're staying with Lady Bonkers."

"She's my aunt," Emma said a little stiffly.

"Sorry about that. It's what my granny calls her. She's known her a long time. The whole family . . . the first wife who died, and the second wife. Granny says that one was pretty nice."

"The second one was my grandmother. She died before I was born. I thought she and my grandfather moved to Connecticut a hundred years ago," Emma said.

"Well, my granny isn't that old. She used to sail one of your grandfather's boats. But she had to stop. When your aunt would come home from boarding school to visit her father, it would make her mad to see old Granny out there on the bay in a sailboat, tacking and coming about and hoisting the sails like an America's Cup winner." The girl threw back her head and laughed. Emma had to smile, too.

"You must be Alberta," she said.

"Call me Bertie," said the girl.

"My aunt said you have a blazing talent with watercolors," Emma said.

"Wow!" cried Bertie. "I can't paint the side of a barn." She stooped to sift through Emma's collection of shells and stones. "I used to make little heaps of things when I first came out here," she said. "Let's go down the beach."

As she walked alongside of Bertie, Emma felt that, at last, her spirit was rising. She imagined it was the way you felt when the sailboat you were in caught the wind.

"Granny and your Aunt Bea don't see each other these days," Bertie told her. "The last time, Granny made her supper because your uncle had to go somewhere. Your aunt never stopped talking about a friend of hers who, she said, was the world's greatest cook. It makes you feel grim, Granny said. You know she's trying to make you feel bad. Like telling you I was so good at painting. Did you show her a watercolor you'd done? That would have set her off. What's that book?"

"I didn't show her anything," said Emma.

She held out the book and Bertie took it quickly but with a gentle hand. Emma liked that. Most kids grabbed things from you. "Pretty interesting," Bertie commented, looking through the pages. "I might have gone on collecting if I'd had this."

"How long do you stay out here?" asked Emma.

"Until school starts," Bertie replied. "My mother and father go to Denmark most summers to visit our relatives. I've never wanted to go with them. But I guess I'll have to next summer. I love it out here with Granny. We have a good time together."

"Look at the sun," Emma said. Both girls halted. The great red ball of fire was sinking behind a line of low hills in the west.

"Are you coming down to the beach tomorrow?" Bertie asked.

"I'm coming down every day, early, even if there's a storm," Emma said. "I like to get out of that house."

"Yeah," Bertie said softly.

7

The Village
by the Sea

WHEN had the idea struck Emma and Bertie? Was
it there all the time they roamed the beach, searching
for shells they could match up with illustrations in
Emma's book? It must have grown slowly, the way
light comes at dawn, and gradually reveals an island
or a hill, a forest, that has been hidden by the dark.

They picked up other things beside shells; blue
and green beach glass roughened by tide and wind
and the abrasion of the sand, bits of wood as smooth
as satin, a buckle from a belt, corks, a few glass
bottles, stones of many shapes, and seaweed dry as
paper, green sea lettuce and rockweed and Irish

moss. There were egg capsules, too, devil's purse black as ink, and the hard little collars where moon snails had lived. There were the shells of worm snails, spirals and corkscrews white as chalk, and sponges which were gray or yellow and crumbly, and the ghostly amber shells of crabs. Some of these things reminded Emma of old musical instruments her father had showed her in a music encyclopedia.

The third morning the two girls met on the beach, Emma handed Bertie what appeared to be a tiny pine tree around three inches tall. It was the tip of a branch she had found near the house. Bertie stuck it in sand beside their collection, which they kept at the foot of the cliff, away from the highest tide line. Emma turned a bottle upside down and stood it near the tree.

"An aquarium," she said.

Bertie picked up the rusty belt buckle. "We'll be able to use this," she said. With a handful of twigs and seaweed, Emma made a cottage. She anchored the belt buckle in the sand against the cottage. "The door," she said. She made two fingers into legs and ran them toward the door. "This is a girl running to the cottage. She's just put her horse in the stable. We can build one of stone."

"We can build a city!" cried Bertie.

"A village," said Emma. "We won't have time for a city."

The idea had come out of the darkness.

Emma went to bed, eager for the night to pass, thinking of the day ahead. Usually, Aunt Bea didn't come downstairs for breakfast. But she might. Emma began to get up so early, Uncle Crispin was still asleep. She left him a note that third morning, saying from now on she'd get her own breakfast.

She had liked Uncle Crispin very much when they'd driven out from New York City. She still liked him but he wasn't the same with her as he had been in the car. In Aunt Bea's presence, he looked worried, his brow furrowed, trying to make her laugh, trying not to be angry when she was mean.

Emma couldn't look at the Monet poster. Aunt Bea kept on talking about the painter as if she owned him, like a piece of land she had inherited. Even when she wasn't there at the dining table, Emma would glimpse the teapot as she went out the door to the porch and feel a kind of coldness steal through her as though the air had grown chill. Aunt Bea's remarks about people were like being punched in the same spot over and over again. You got a kind of ache just listening to her, and the ache didn't go away.

91

Lunch was hard. "What does cold-blooded mean?" Aunt Bea shouted imperiously at Uncle Crispin who was fixing himself coffee in the kitchen. "Just what it says, Bea," he replied mildly. There were times when he didn't answer her questions, when his mouth remained tightly closed.

Something was always going on between them, Emma reflected. They never left each alone unless Uncle Crispin was playing his violin or Aunt Bea was glued to the television set.

Emma had peeked into all the rooms except their bedroom. Uncle Crispin used one for his practicing. There were shelves holding music there, and a music stand, but the other rooms were empty except for the smallest, where a large old-fashioned trunk stood in the middle of the floor.

"Why is a senator more important than a representative?" Aunt Bea called from the living room.

"For mercy's sake, Bea—" replied Uncle Crispin in an exasperated voice. "You grew up in this country. A senator has a larger constituency, serves a longer term and has more power. There are only two senators for each state—"

Aunt Bea must have kicked a teacup on the floor. Emma, snatching a cracker and an apple in the kitchen, heard it shatter.

"I don't fill my head with unimportant details," Aunt Bea cried. "Now look what you made me do!"

Emma fled to the beach.

It wasn't so easy when Uncle Crispin was out giving a violin lesson at the time when Emma came up from the beach to grab a bite.

Aunt Bea, drinking tea, the table covered with wool and writing paper, said, "Oh, for heaven's sake! Don't just run in and out. Visit with me. What's so fascinating on the beach? I suppose you've met that girl next door. Sit down and eat a civilized lunch." She was scratching at her fingers. Emma glimpsed a sheet of paper covered with handwriting, the letters like plump balloons.

"Bertie is waiting for me," she said uneasily.

"So you did meet her!" her aunt accused. "Bertie! You ought to advise her to change her name. She'll end up being called Bert, the truck driver. Look! I found this in my desk and I thought you'd love it!"

She was holding out a comic book, although the cover didn't look like any comic book Emma had ever seen. She wanted to run out of the room. Aunt Bea continued to hold up the book, her mouth smiling, but something hopeless about her eyes, like someone watching a fire burn up her house. Emma reached for the book. Aunt Bea snatched it away. "No, no. *I* want to show it to you."

Reluctantly, Emma stood beside her. Aunt Bea's reddened finger pointed at every object in the cartoons: a brick, a small ramshackle jailhouse, a path with a single cactus growing beside it. Emma had to admit to herself that it was funny.

"You see, it's always the same story," Aunt Bea explained happily. "A triangle—Krazy Kat, Offissa Pup, and Ignatz Mouse. Look at the drawing itself. Wonderful! There's nothing to match it these days. The mouse always ends up in jail for throwing bricks, but he's the winner! That's because Krazy Kat loves him so."

"I have to go, Aunt Bea," Emma said.

Aunt Bea bowed her head over the comic book. She looked up to gaze at her poster. She poured tea. Then she said slowly, "This is more valuable than anything you've got on the beach. Well—then go!"

Another day when Uncle Crispin was out, she had fixed Emma an enormous sandwich. "Look at that! It's for you. And I've made some China green tea, very mild, suitable for someone your age." She had set a place for Emma at the table with a huge ragged linen napkin and a heavy silver fork.

The sandwich was delicious, but Emma knew she would have to pay for it.

"Did I ever tell you about the time Crispin and I were in Sicily?" she asked in a high, rather silly voice. "It was winter when there were no tourists. They were home where they belong. We had driven along the southern coast . . . look, here's a map I got out for you . . . and night fell. In Messina, we had heard of a marvelous hotel. We stopped there. We could see one dim light somewhere in what must have been the lobby. Can you imagine! Night—in Sicily—in winter! What looked like an empty hotel! We started to get out of the car when a pack of monstrous wild dogs came out of the darkness, howling, snapping their great jaws."

Emma stared at her, her interest caught despite her wish to go. She remembered what Bertie had said when she told her about Krazy Kat, and how her aunt had tried to make her stay. "Granny says she goes nuts when he's away."

"We sat there all night," Aunt Bea was saying, her eyes boring into Emma's. "And in the morning, my dear, the dogs were still there, waiting for us, their big meal of the day. At last some peasant came along and shooed them away with sticks and stones, and the donkey hee-hawed and your poor Uncle Crispin and I got out of the car like two stone statues."

"That's a good story," Emma said. "But I have to go now."

"I have another," Aunt Bea said, her eyes getting glassy, "about a cliff of birds on the west coast of Ireland."

That day, Emma was rescued by Uncle Crispin's unexpected arrival; a student was ill, a lesson cancelled, and Emma set free.

Every evening, her mother called. Each day there was a new event. Daddy was out of Intensive Care and in his own room. Daddy walked. He ate two tangerines for dessert and all the chicken. "Oh!" cried her mother, "you know how white-faced he's been for so long? Now he looks as if he'd just taken a walk on a frosty day. You should see the color in his face!"

The knowledge that her father was really getting well sank into her. Often, during the hours with Bertie, she never gave him a thought.

"YESTERDAY evening, I just touched a key on the piano," she was telling Bertie. "Uncle Crispin was making supper. She was in the living room and could hardly have heard that note. But she yelled, 'Don't thump!' "

"Never mind her," Bertie said. The day was hot and she'd taken a quick dip in the water. Her freckled shoulders gleamed and her yellow hair was thick with salt and water. "We have to make the school today."

In four days, they had built eleven houses out of pebbles, shells, seaweed, and bits of wood. "Abodes," Bertie called them. Pine boughs and oak twigs and sea lavender formed hedges; and from plants plucked from the tangle that grew along the cliff edge, they made gardens. The mayor's house was made of sand dollars roofed with pine cones. The house of the only rich family in their village was built of oyster shells. The main street, which went from one end of the village to the other, was formed of white bubble shells. Slipper shell paths wound around the gardens. The blue and green sea glass made fish ponds and a skylight for a painter's studio. The village center was marked by a large dried starfish—a compass of the sea, Emma said.

"I like the painter's studio best," Bertie said, "the painter with the blazing talent." She laughed. "As long as he doesn't set his house on fire."

"We don't have any stores," Emma noted.

"Let's not," Bertie suggested. "And no dentist's office."

"How big do you think it is?" Emma asked her.

Bertie paced along the stone wall they had built around the whole village. "About twelve feet long," she said. She had offered to bring down some old doll's house furniture, but Emma said they should only use things they found on the beach.

When they knelt on the sand and saw the bits of glass shine, and a breeze touched the little trees and hedges, they agreed that their village looked more real than if it had been life-sized. All around them was the lovely debris of the beach, all the things they had turned into abodes and streets and gardens.

"But I think we have to have a doctor's office," Emma said, "in case someone gets sick."

Bertie knew about Emma's father. She didn't disagree. "I think we ought to have an inn, too," she said. "Granny took me to lunch last October to a town on the Hudson River with this place that had been a revolutionary tavern. It was old-fashioned and cozy, like our houses."

"We could have a one-room schoolhouse," Emma said. "And we could make a jungle gym in the yard out of twigs."

"The inn or the school first?" asked Bertie.

"The doctor's office," Emma said. "But it could be a house so that, when you have to have a shot, you could look out on a rose bush."

"Fat chance," remarked Bertie. "Doctors *like* you to stare at white walls and steel furniture—otherwise you might not be so scared."

They would walk down the beach, sometimes together, sometimes each girl on her own, looking for treasure. The hours flowed like the waves of the bay, unmarked each one. They never had a special thing they were looking for. It seemed to work better that way—they had better luck when they were just mooning around. Bertie had sharp eyes. She would hold her head sideways like a shorebird looking for a sand shrimp, pounce, and come up with a prize. Only the yellow or white plastic bottles that washed up on the beach were absolutely useless.

8

A Dog, a Deer

FOR several evenings, Emma had not bothered to mark time on the calendar she had made. When, one night, she remembered, she saw there were only six days left of her stay on Peconic Bay.

As she sat down to supper the next evening, Aunt Bea leaned over her plate, her head bowed, her arms clasped, and said, "I don't think she should spend so much time in the water, Crispin. She's losing weight."

"Do you stay in the water a long time?" Uncle Crispin asked Emma. "Though I hardly think she'll shrink from bathing, Bea," he added.

"Just now and then to cool off," Emma replied. She hoped there would be no more questions. She felt apprehensive about mentioning the village.

Aunt Bea rocked back and forth a moment, staring into her plate. "What is this, Crispin? Some sort of Mulligan stew? A tribute to the Irish?"

"This stew has nothing to do with the Irish," Uncle Crispin said, smiling as though his wife had said something clever.

"Everything English has to do with the Irish," said Aunt Bea.

Uncle Crispin's smile vanished. "What I made is a tribute to the good quality of the vegetables and meat that survived my unskilled hands," he said in an exasperated voice.

Aunt Bea looked at Emma. "We're having an argument," she said with a touch of gaiety.

"An argument," Uncle Crispin repeated. "Good. Then we can arrive at a peaceful settlement."

"An argument is a fight," Aunt Bea said. "It doesn't lead to peace."

"Of course not. Unless one wants peace," Uncle Crispin retorted.

In the silence which followed, Emma ate a carrot. It was not quite cooked, and it crunched loudly.

"Well?" Aunt Bea questioned her. "What about

it? If you don't swim, what are you two girls up to?"

"We're building a—" she hesitated for a long moment—"a little village."

Aunt Bea burst into hectic laughter. "The poor beach . . . no one lets it be!" she cried. "They build houses on it, rake it, cover it with radios and cheap ugly towels . . . the poor—"

The telephone rang.

"Do answer it, Emma," Uncle Crispin said. "I'm sure it's for you."

"What a disciplined mother," Aunt Bea said softly.

Oh, why does Aunt Bea have to comment on everything, Emma thought as she went to the phone. There was nearly always a sharpness in her voice, like a razor blade hidden in cotton.

"Hello," she said, more loudly than she'd meant to.

"Emma?" inquired a familiar voice.

"Daddy!"

"This is my first phone call," he said. "I'm sitting up wearing the sweater your mother made me."

"The one with the one sleeve longer than the other?"

He laughed and said, "Yes."

Her throat seemed to close, and for a moment, she was unable to speak.

"Emma, dear. I know how glad you are. Do you know how glad I am? Today, I walked nearly half a mile along the hospital corridor. They really ought to plant a few trees. First hospitals scare the daylights out of you. Then they bore the daylights out of you."

Her heart thumping, Emma thought: Scare you to death. . . .

"I'm coming home in two days," he said. "And Mom's coming to get you Monday."

"Is it all right?" she said breathlessly. "Is your heart all right now?"

"It's pretty good," he replied. "Emma, I can draw a deep breath. It's wonderful. It's like drawing up a pail of fresh, cold water from a well."

She drew a deep breath herself. "Just like that," he said. "Tell me—how has it been? I've thought of you whenever they weren't fiddling around with me here. How is the terror?"

She lowered her voice. "They've been arguing about *stew*," she told him. "Daddy, she's so mean! And, Daddy—did she used to drink a lot of brandy?"

He didn't answer quickly. She listened to him breathing, so happy at the even sound of it, she nearly forgot what she'd asked him.

Finally, he said, "Yes, she did. But she stopped.

I admired her for that. But she has a habit of resentment. It's a kind of addiction, too, like brandy."

"Is she especially mad at your mother because of the house in Connecticut?" Emma asked in a whisper. She had heard the sound of a chair being pushed across the floor.

"I think so," he said. "She's been angry at my mother for a thousand years. It's pretty hopeless being mad at ghosts." He paused, then, his voice filled with concern, asked her, "Has she been terrible to you?"

Emma thought a moment. "No, it's not that," she said.

"Emma, your supper is getting cold, Crispin's wonderful stew!" shouted Aunt Bea, her voice carrying from the dining room.

"I heard that," Emma's father said. "She always could say *wonderful* so it could slice you in half. Never mind. It's hard to believe, but she doesn't care what the target is—she wants to feel the stones leaving her hand—it won't be long, my duck."

"I'm so glad, Daddy," Emma said feelingly.

"So am I," he said.

On her way back to the dining room, she passed the long table. Uncle Crispin's violin was elsewhere, but behind a pile of music books, she saw the tiny plastic deer. Without thinking she grabbed it up and stuck it in her pocket.

"It was Daddy," she said to the two of them, sitting silently at the dining table. "Mom's coming to get me Monday. That's a day early."

"He must be doing very well indeed," Uncle Crispin observed. He looked quite tired, Emma thought.

"You might try to disguise how happy you are to get away from me," Aunt Bea said, pouting.

"Oh, it's not that!" protested Emma. "It's going home, seeing them. It's—"

"All right, all right . . ." muttered Aunt Bea. "I know that."

"I'M going home Monday," Emma told Bertie.

"That's only four days," Bertie said. "And I think we have to have a library, and a church for everyone, no special kind."

"We ought to have a little forest, too," Emma said, "behind the village, at the foot of the cliff, so that people can go on picnics in the summer. There has to be a wild place."

"That's a good idea," Bertie agreed.

"I have a wild creature to put in our forest," Emma said, showing Bertie the deer.

"Did you find that on the beach?" asked Bertie.

"No," Emma replied.

"But you said we should use only what we found lying around on the sand," Bertie recalled.

"I know I did," Emma said. Since she couldn't explain to herself why she wanted the deer to be part of what they had made, she could hardly explain it to Bertie. The deer was the right size, but she didn't think that was the whole reason. The doll's house furniture Bertie had offered would have been, too. She felt cranky suddenly as though Bertie was arguing about the deer—which she wasn't. But they weren't building doll's houses.

The village had taken on a life of its own. The tiny twigs and branches looked like real trees when they swayed in a breeze. The street of luminous shells gleamed. In the gardens behind the houses, the hedges and flowers stirred, and the studio skylight often seemed lit from within. It wasn't a place built for dolls with their hard little bodies and frozen faces.

She sighed. "The deer comes from a brandy bottle," she said to Bertie. "They had a big fight about it."

Bertie nodded as though she knew all about that. Emma supposed she did. By now, they knew each other's feelings about Aunt Bea. They didn't talk about her much. When they did, Emma didn't feel uneasy as she had at first. In fact, it was a relief. Yesterday, she had mentioned to Bertie how Aunt Bea only looked really happy when she was watching a television program.

Bertie had said, "Granny thinks she's usually happy when she's watching all her enemies."

"Who are her enemies?" Emma had asked.

"Oh—everybody," Bertie had said vaguely. "Everybody out there in the world."

Remembering that, Emma said, "Your Granny must really hate her." They were gathering round stones for the library.

"Oh, no," Bertie said. "She thinks she's funny. But she said she supposed she wouldn't find her so funny if she had to live with her."

"We could use a horseshoe crab for the church," Emma suggested. "Its tail would make a good spire."

They couldn't find a horseshoe crab so Bertie said they could build a Greek temple for people to go into and be quiet for a while. "That's a good idea," Emma said, "and we can use sticks for columns and one of those flat, slaty stones for the roof."

They set off on a search. Emma wasn't cranky anymore. She was thinking only of what they might find, half-buried in the sand, waiting to be discovered.

On Friday, Aunt Bea was alone when Emma went to the house to get a glass of milk. She insisted Emma look at some things of hers she had been saving for a surprise.

Moving heavily, panting a little, she led Emma up the stairs to one of the rooms Emma had looked into. Inside it was the old-fashioned trunk.

"It's from the Civil War," Aunt Bea said proudly. "It belonged to my great-grandfather who was an officer, of course. See his initials? K.B.? And here are spots of melted wax from the candles he stuck on it so he could write letters to his wife, whom he adored. Now . . ." and she flung open the lid. A smell of must and age, of old cloth, filled Emma's nostrils. Her eyes widened at the quantity of laces and silks, frail as moths' wings, that billowed up.

Aunt Bea stared at her triumphantly. "These marvelous things belonged to his wife," she said. "Look at the tiny stitches! Look!" She held up a garment whose seams were nearly invisible. "No machine could do that," Aunt Bea said. She picked up a large fan, opened it, fluttered it in front of her face and

109

peered over it at Emma. "This is beyond price," she said. "Irreplaceable!" Reverently, she put back what she'd taken from the trunk.

"Your grandmother tried to steal this," she said harshly. "But I wouldn't let her. This trunk is my one triumph!"

"It's beautiful," Emma said desperately, feeling she might not get out of the room with its dry ghost smell of clothes, the possession of a vanished woman, the trunk sitting there like a tomb. Anger had pinched Aunt Bea's face. Her eyes narrowed as she looked in a corner of the room as though the person who had enraged her was standing there, visible only to her.

Suddenly she smiled, not turning her head. "I suppose you want to get back to your mud pies with old Bert," she said scornfully.

Emma started to protest that they weren't making mud pies, that "old Bert" was Bertie, tall and thin and sweet. But she said nothing. She had suddenly noticed that Aunt Bea was wearing not one but two of the old robes she had found in the thrift shop and the buckles were missing from the sandals on her feet. Her face was flushed as though she'd been running. Maybe she didn't drink brandy anymore, but something in her mind was making her drunk.

"I'll go now," Emma said quietly. She left the room, then the house.

Bertie was waiting, standing at the edge of the village, her hands on her hips. Emma began to tell her about the trunk, but Bertie held up her hand. "Wait! Just look!" She pointed at the beginning of the main street. Emma saw an animal print. The artist's studio had been knocked apart, and there was a trail of paw marks leading to the forest.

"Oh!" she exclaimed.

"A dog," Bertie said grimly. "While I went up for lunch with Granny, someone took their dog for a walk or let it out of the house. Can you beat that? It's all wrecked."

"It isn't wrecked," Emma cried. "It's a little shaky. And that's all. Come on. We can fix it."

There were tears on Bertie's cheeks. Emma forgot about Aunt Bea and her old, sour anger.

"Bertie, it isn't that bad. Honestly. Look, he only ran over a little bit of the street and a couple of the houses."

Bertie didn't move. Emma squatted down and picked up the studio skylight. "Come on, help me," she said. "Things always happen. It isn't just our beach."

It didn't take long to repair the damage, to smooth away the dog's knobby paw marks.

"I suppose it could have been worse," Bertie admitted after they saw that everything was back where it had been. "The dog probably thought it was a public facility for dogs."

That afternoon, they finished the library. It looked to Emma like the one built of fieldstone in the town near the cottage in upstate New York.

Bertie found a large flat slab of slate for their temple almost as soon as she started looking for one. They had a lovely time making the forest, drawing with a small stick a network of tiny paths leading to a clearing for picnics.

"Tomorrow, we'll make everything perfect," Emma said. "We ought to build a fireplace in the clearing so people can cook there."

"We need a sign for the inn," Bertie remembered. "I could print one when we decide on the name."

"Maybe we'll find something tomorrow," Emma said.

They took a short swim. It had been a good day's work. Emma had even liked fixing the damage done by the dog.

Just before they parted, Bertie said, "We could call the inn *The Sign of the Deer*."

Emma said they ought to think of something else. She didn't tell Bertie, but she wanted the deer to be hidden in the forest.

"We're lucky there haven't been any high tides," Bertie said as Emma started up the stairs. "Just one, and everything would have been washed out to the bay."

Looking down on the village, Emma felt exhilarated. They had built it in a place full of dangers: tides, a storm, wandering animals, anything could have destroyed it. But it was there, smaller than life, but just as strong.

For supper that night, there were scrambled eggs and sliced tomatoes. Uncle Crispin had had too many lessons to do much shopping or cooking. Aunt Bea piled up a saucer with ice cream. She grinned at Emma as she ate great spoonfuls of it.

"It's divine," she murmured.

"How's your beach project?" Uncle Crispin asked.

"It's great," Emma replied. "When we finish it tomorrow, will you come down and look at it?" She was looking at Uncle Crispin, but because Aunt Bea's grin had seemed so friendly, she turned to her and asked, "Will you come, too?"

"I can't wait to see it," Uncle Crispin said. "I remember building a tree house when I was a boy. A friend and I. His name was Bob. Yes . . . Bob and I built a wonderful roost, like Tarzan's. It was the best time of my life."

"Really," Aunt Bea said in a rather buttery voice.

"As a child," Uncle Crispin said.

"I read and painted," Aunt Bea said, holding her head stiffly. "I never did things like that, sticking my hands in dirt or nailing old sticks together and pretending I was doing something important."

"Oh, Bea . . ." Uncle Crispin said in a hopeless way.

She giggled suddenly. "Oh, Crispin! Can I have a touch more of ice cream? It's *so* delicious!"

Emma's father phoned just as they finished the last of the ice cream. He sounded calm and as if he were at home. Some friends were coming to visit him that evening so their conversation was a short one. It felt to Emma almost as though it was the time before he had become sick, even though he was still in the hospital.

As she started back through the living room to help Uncle Crispin clean up the supper dishes, she heard him say, "There, there, my dear . . ."

She paused near the fireplace.

114

Aunt Bea's voice was soft, murmuring. Then it rose a little. "My trunk . . ." Emma heard. "My mother . . ." Then it surged like a wave at its crest. "Oh, Crispin," she said. "When I woke up this morning, I thought my heart was broken!"

There was silence. Emma went to the entrance of the dining room. Uncle Crispin was crouched next to Aunt Bea, his arms around her waist. She rested her cheek on his head, the fall of her gun-metal hair hiding his ear and neck. They both looked up at Emma, their faces bewildered as though they hadn't known anyone else was in their house.

9

Vandal

"YOU won't believe this even when you see it!" cried Bertie who was waiting on the beach for Emma Sunday morning.

She held out a two-inch square of balsa wood. "Careful!" she warned as Emma took it. "It's almost falling apart."

One side of the square was blank; on the other, faded but legible, was one word: *Lodgings*.

"It was way down there," Bertie said, pointing at a spot on the beach where several people were pushing a large raft into the water. "It must have been in the sand since last summer . . . from some kid's

117

building set. . . . I was walking around there early this morning. I dropped my apple, and when I bent down to pick it up, I saw a plastic house roof. Underneath it was the sign."

Emma thought the sign itself was a sign that they had finished their village.

Bertie sharpened a twig on a stone and threaded it through the balsa wood and stuck it in the sand in front of their inn.

"Is it really done, do you think?" she asked Emma wistfully.

"Just in time," said Emma. "But look. Some of the stones in the library have slipped. We can fix that and check on every cottage and the doctor's office and the temple. Everything."

They spent an hour or so doing what was unnecessary, for the village was, they agreed, now as perfect as it could be.

Wind had shifted sand; some of the hedges were down, twigs fallen on paths. The village had taken on a weathered look, that of an old, old place which no highway would ever lead to, which you might only discover if you were riding a horse one afternoon by the sea. You would give the horse its head; it would wander over the crest of a low hill and, looking down, you would see the village in the sleepy, sun-dazed quietness.

That was what Emma was thinking in a dreaming way. As if Bertie had sensed what was in Emma's mind, she said, "We should have built more stables for horses."

"You have to stop somewhere," Emma replied. "We'd end up trying to build the world."

"We did," Bertie declared. "Granny wants to see it. But her sciatica is so bad, she really can't come down the stairs. I told her I'd take some pictures with her camera."

The hearings Aunt Bea had been watching weren't on television that day. She was in her usual chair at the table. She was wearing a somber gray dress whose skirt reached her ankles. Around her neck was a necklace of small luminous blue stones which she twisted and curled about her fingers.

"We've finished our village by the sea," Emma said as Uncle Crispin set before her a plate of lettuce and slices of avocado for her lunch.

"Whatever you've made—it isn't by the sea," Aunt Bea said sharply. "It's by the bay."

"I'm eager to see it," Uncle Crispin said quickly. "Bea, let me fix you something. Soup? A sandwich?"

"I have no appetite today," Aunt Bea said, tightening the necklace around her throat.

"But you'll come down to see the village?" he asked. "It would do you good."

"It wouldn't do me a bit of good," Aunt Bea said, looking up at her poster. She let go of the blue stones and smiled to herself. "I can see all the beach I need to ever see in my Monet. I haven't time for such excursions."

She shook her head slowly as if everything was too much for her. She's telling herself a story, Emma thought, all about what she has to put up with, she and Monet.

Uncle Crispin sighed. "We'll go down, Emma, as soon as you're finished. We can do the dishes later."

"Don't expect me to clean up after you," Aunt Bea said shrilly.

"No one expects any such thing," retorted Uncle Crispin.

After they left the house and were going down the stairs, Emma felt for a moment transparent with happiness, as though it were a light shining through her.

Even though she would have to part from Bertie, she was going home tomorrow. The days which had, at first, seemed to stretch before her like a road with no end, had gone so fast she had been taken by surprise when she realized her time by the bay was just about over.

Bertie was down below, running back and forth near the water. When she saw them, she shouted, "Good!"

The three of them stood together by the stone wall around the village.

"What a piece of work!" exclaimed Uncle Crispin. "It could be a little corner by the sea in Dorset or Cornwall in England. Look at the gardens! You two are wonders!" He stooped down. "What a lovely place to live!"

Emma and Bertie smiled at each other.

"Have you named it?" Uncle Crispin asked, standing up. He was peering at the forest. Emma felt a start of fear. She didn't want him to see the deer.

"Look at the library," she suggested hurriedly, "the one with brown stones. No, we haven't named it yet."

"Just the sort of library where one would like to spend a drowsy afternoon," Uncle Crispin said. "Well—it is the most extraordinary thing you've done. . . . I thought it would be like a large sand castle. I had no idea it was such a serious project."

After he had gone back to the house, Bertie took

a number of pictures of the village. "When I see you back in the city in September, I'll give you copies of whatever turns out right," she promised.

"If a teacher asks us to write a composition about what we did this summer—" Emma began.

"—we can do an illustrated one," Bertie said.

"Let's take a walk," Emma said. They lingered, though, by the village, looking at their work. Emma felt a little sad. "It was doing it that was so great," she said. They started off.

"It was all I thought about," Bertie said. "I think I even dreamed about it every night."

"I'm glad my aunt didn't see it," Emma said. "She would have told us it wasn't up to Paris or London— or even Albany."

The large raft was now anchored a hundred yards or so out on the bay.

"Look!" said Bertie. "There's the family that rents the house next to Granny's." Emma saw at least five children paddling in the little waves. Two grown-ups were opening a huge yellow beach umbrella.

"The summer has begun," commented Bertie. "Pretty soon, the beach will be filled with people."

"How long will our village last?" wondered Emma.

"Who knows? The main thing is—we made it," responded Bertie.

They walked for a long time until they could no longer see the stairs that led up the cliff to their houses. The cliff fell away. A ridge of low-lying dunes took its place. On the other side of them was a large pond upon which three swans floated like meringues.

"It's beautiful," Emma commented. "I'm glad I got to see this part of the beach."

"We ought to name the village," Bertie said. "Yeah, it is pretty here. Those swans come back to the pond every year, I've heard."

"How about *Swan Haven*?" Emma suggested.

"Why not *Deer Haven*?" Bertie asked. "We really do have a deer in the forest—not a swan. It's more true."

Emma hesitated. But after all, only she and Bertie would know the name of their village. "Okay," she agreed.

BEFORE supper Emma packed her suitcase and her shopping bag. She glanced at her diary before she dropped it on top of the puzzles she hadn't done, the books she hadn't read. She ought to write something down, but it seemed impossible. How could she write about the eagerness with which she raced down the stairs to the beach every morning? How could she describe the moment when Bertie handed her the balsa wood sign? Perhaps there are no words for what is perfect, she thought. Even counting the summers with her father and mother at the place in upstate New York, she couldn't think of anything in her life that had held such delight as those hours with Bertie. Nothing Aunt Bea had said had touched them.

Aunt Bea was almost silent at supper. Uncle Crispin had broiled a steak and made rather lumpy mashed potatoes.

"Quite like nursery potatoes," he remarked. "We used to count the lumps. Whoever had the most got an extra share of pudding."

"Who is *we*?" asked Aunt Bea gruffly.

"Oh—a friend who might be visiting. Bea, I do wish you'd look at what these children made. It is simply magical!"

Aunt Bea stared down at her plate.

"They even built a library and a Greek temple!" he went on.

Aunt Bea rose abruptly and padded out to the kitchen in her beaded white moccasins. Soon, Emma heard the kettle boiling, and Aunt Bea appeared a moment later with a cup of tea. As she sat down, she said, "Crispin, I think I should like to go to Provence in the fall. I'm tired of this meager beach, those hordes who come out here every year."

"If we can manage it, Bea," Uncle Crispin said. "Travel is so expensive."

"Don't look to me for that problem," Aunt Bea said angrily. "I have nothing . . . nothing."

She glared at Emma as though everything was her fault. She drank from her cup, her eyes still on Emma, but the glow of anger in her eyes died away. When she put down the cup, she muttered, "Oh I know we can't go. . . . It was just a thought."

After supper and the dishes, Emma went to the living room. Aunt Bea was on the sofa in front of the television set.

"Shall I watch a movie with you?" Emma asked timidly. It was her last evening, after all.

"Who said I was going to watch a movie?" asked her aunt. She suddenly snatched up the channel changer and hit the button so quickly, a blur of stations floated by.

Emma sat down next to her.

"Ah," sighed Aunt Bea, dropping the changer on the sofa between them. Emma watched as people speaking with English accents moved around a large kitchen. "That's the cook, Mrs. Bridges," announced

Aunt Bea more to the room than to Emma. "This is the second time I've watched this series. I adore it. Crispin? If you don't get a haircut soon, you'll look exactly like Mrs. Bridges."

"Oh, dear," Uncle Crispin said from his table. "If I could only cook as well as she does!"

Aunt Bea laughed loudly. "It's all a joke," she said. "They give her a bowl and a whisk and she turns out a seven-course dinner for the king of England. If you were like me, you'd see that everything is a joke."

Emma got up then and said good night without looking at her aunt or her uncle. As she went up to her room, she thought of how glad she was that she was leaving.

The moon's rays made her room so light, Emma didn't turn on the lamp. She knelt by the window, her elbows on the sill. A breeze was stirring the trees. The balsa sign that read *Lodgings* would be waving like a small banner. A night traveler would see it by the light of the moon and be comforted. She imagined herself walking down the main street toward the starfish. Which house would be hers? She chose the one made of sand dollars. Way out on the bay, she saw a tiny light. Someone must be night fishing.

She would miss the water, its smell, the whisper of waves.

When she finally got into bed, she fell asleep at once.

~~~~~~~~~~~~~~~~~~~~

EMMA sat straight up in her bed. What had she heard? A soft shushing sound as though heavy cloth were being dragged along the hall. Then she realized it must be Aunt Bea in her moccasins. She held her breath, and in that instant, the sound faded away. She turned on the lamp. She felt she'd slept ten hours but the alarm clock showed it was only three a.m. She tried to read but couldn't concentrate. She began to feel sleepy; the book slipped from the bed and hit the floor with a thud. Her eyes flew open. She sat straight up. There was a gasping, rasping noise just outside her door. It passed in a few seconds. The silence returned.

Now she was fully awake. On a sudden impulse, she got up, pulled on her jeans over her pajamas and shoved her feet into sandals. She would take a look at the village by night. She would know it in all its hours. As she went through the small foyer, she took the flashlight from the shelf.

From the porch, the dark waters of the bay glinted as though pricked by starlight. The islands were invisible, and the bay seemed to flow into the sky itself. Emma took the stairs slowly, feeling the tickle of the long sea grass against her ankles.

The sand was cold. She turned on the flashlight and looked down.

The village was wrecked. Stones and shells, seaweed and glass, all that had made the abodes, the temple, the library, the school, were scattered about, and hillocks of sand covered paths and gardens. She bent to pick up the starfish compass, ripped in half. Near where the doctor's house had been was the plastic deer. Two large stones lay close by, one of the deer's legs crushed between them. She knelt, holding herself up with one hand. With the other, she shone the flashlight close to the sand. She saw several tiny beads, blue and white and red. The throbbing of her heart sounded like a great alarm gong that should wake up all people who lived along the cliff. She grabbed the beads and waved her hand to shake away the sand that clung to them. She turned off the flashlight and stood in the dark, looking up at the sky. The blackness was like a substance she was swallowing.

It seemed only a moment later that she found

herself on the long porch among the rocking chairs
that huddled there like old, old people. Through the
window, she saw a ray of light on the dining table.
She went inside. Uncle Crispin stood in the kitchen
doorway holding a cup of tea.

"Emma?" he questioned.

She began to cry. She put the flashlight on the
table and held one hand against her mouth. In the
other, she felt the hard little beads.

"Why, Emma!" he said in alarm.

She looked at him and opened her fist. He peered
down at the beads, his face uncomprehending. She
couldn't speak yet. She looked around the dining
room, into its shadowed corners. She was looking
for something; she didn't know what it was. Then
her glance rested on the Monet poster.

"Emma—tell me!" Uncle Crispin said urgently.

"She smashed our village," Emma sobbed. "It
looks bombed. There's nothing left. . . ."

"She?"

But he knew who *she* was. Emma could tell by
the way his eyes narrowed, his mouth shut tight. He
looked grim.

"Show me the beads," he said. She held out her
hand. He touched them one by one. Suddenly, she
snatched her hand away, shook it so the beads

dropped onto the floor. She went quickly to the poster, her hands raised to rip it from the wall.

"Emma! No!" he ordered her.

The desire to destroy it was so strong she thought she could feel it tearing in her hands.

"Don't touch it," he said. "I don't care about the poster. I care about you."

She turned back to him.

He had put the cup of tea down and drawn out a chair. "Sit here," he said.

Her arms fell to her side. She felt weak. She did as he said.

"I can't explain anything," he said in a low voice. "I don't ask you to forgive her. One of the tutors I had as a boy was much given to adages. Do you know what an adage is?"

She shook her head. She was barely listening to him, thinking of the destroyed village, of the place where it had stood which would, in a few days, look just like any other part of the beach.

"An adage is a way of summing up a kind of wisdom in a few words . . . like 'haste makes waste' or 'a stitch in time saves nine.' They're boring, I know, but so often true. This tutor I was speaking about always spoke in adages. I recall a few. One was this: 'Envy's a coal comes hissing hot from hell.' "

He was staring at her. His face was partly in shadow, the kitchen light falling on his white hair.

"Emma," he called softly as though she were far away. "I'm the only person Bea doesn't envy. That is because I'm married to her. Do you understand what that means?"

She heard herself sigh.

"It means she knows about herself," he went on. "That hot coal is inside her. She feels it more terribly than anyone else. She feels helpless—that's why she says those dreadful things."

"She did something this time," Emma said. "She didn't just say something."

"Yes," he said. "You can't imagine how funny and nice she can be . . . when we're alone here."

Emma felt terribly tired. She didn't want to hear anything more from Uncle Crispin. "She hates me so," she said, thinking that would put an end to the talk. Then she could go to bed and sleep.

"No!" he said fiercely. "It's not you she hates. It's the world. She feels left out."

"It would have blown away in a storm," Emma said. "Or a high tide. People would've stepped on

131

it." She looked up at the Monet poster. She remembered her aunt saying, "the silliness of human beings against the force of nature." But human beings were a force of nature, too.

"I was taking her a cup of tea," Uncle Crispin said sadly. "She is very unhappy. I didn't know what was wrong. She'll regret what she's done forever."

Emma didn't quite believe that. All she wanted now was to be in her room. The morning was near.

"You're going home today," he said. "Listen. You were so happy building your village. You mustn't forget that."

The skin on her cheeks felt tight with dried tears.

"I guess I won't," she said. She got up and left the dining room, aware that he continued to stand next to the table, perhaps looking at the chair where she had sat.

10

Home

〜〜〜〜〜〜〜〜〜〜〜〜〜〜〜〜
ΨΨΨΨΨ

WHEN Emma awoke, her eyes felt grainy as though someone had flung sand at them. The sky was as gray as a camp blanket. For the first time, she noticed the chipped paint on the window frames, a long crack that ran the width of the ceiling, a thin layer of dust on the floor. There was a large yellow stain on the braided rug, and dust had gathered around its edges, a tide of dust that would cover it after she had gone and the room closed up as though she'd never been in it.

The silent house, the grayness of the morning that seemed to press up against the grimy windows, made her feel that everything had stopped—she had felt that way before on certain rainy days when she hadn't wanted to get up, dress, when the day ahead was like a long, dreary test for which she wasn't prepared.

She looked at the alarm clock. Time hadn't stopped. It was nearly ten, the hour when she and Bertie had agreed to meet. She got out of bed, listening. She didn't think she could have gone into the hall if she'd heard them.

But she must get down to the beach before Bertie saw the havoc. Why was it that she felt ashamed when it was her aunt who had done the awful thing?

She tiptoed to the bathroom, which Uncle Crispin must have straightened up. When she was dressed, she went back to the hall. She heard a faint murmur of voices and movement from their bedroom, and, as she went down the stairs, a soft padding of moccasined feet, Aunt Bea going to destroy the bathroom, she guessed.

There was scum on the tea in a cup on the dining room table. Uncle Crispin must have forgotten to take it to Aunt Bea after Emma had told him what had happened. She stepped on something hard. It was a blue bead. What had Uncle Crispin said to Aunt Bea when he went upstairs?

It was windy outdoors. The bay looked thick as porridge. Emma didn't pause at the place where the village had been, but went to the stairs that led to Bertie's house. She sat down on the bottom step, pushing her feet into the sand until they were hidden.

How would she tell her?

She couldn't tell Bertie what her father would have called a bare-faced lie. And how could she look at Aunt Bea, at those great doll's eyes, and smile? Could something so dreadful just disappear inside of smiles and talk without a word being said?

She felt a hand on her shoulder and turned her head to look at it, a brown hand with strong, long fingers.

"Bertie," she said, "you didn't make a sound."

"Practice," said Bertie. "Let's go see our village."

"No! Wait!" Emma said, grabbing Bertie's hand. "I have to tell you something."

Bertie sat down on the step below. Emma looked at her long golden braid bound by a rubber band, its tasselled end like a burst of yellow milkweed.

"We could take a swim," Bertie suggested. "The water doesn't look so great. When is your mother coming to get you?"

"Bertie, there is no village—it's gone—everything is gone," Emma said, speaking so quickly, her words ran together.

Bertie turned. She stared at Emma, her eyes narrowing. Without a word, she jumped up and ran to the place where the village had been. Emma sat still, watching her.

Bertie crouched. She reached across the sand and picked something up, looked at it, tossed it away. She stood up and kicked the sand, then raised her arms straight up in the air as though she were about to take a dive. She walked back slowly to Emma, her head down.

"That was no dog," she said.

"No," Emma said.

"There are a couple of kids down the beach who could have done it. They're always tearing up everything."

Emma drew a deep breath. "No. It wasn't them," she said. "It was *her*."

Bertie's eyebrows lifted. "Lady Bonkers?" she breathed.

Emma nodded.

"But why?" cried Bertie.

"I don't know. Maybe because my uncle said it was so wonderful." He had praised it too much, she

136

thought to herself, but how could it have been just that? "I don't know," she repeated.

Emma got up and the two of them walked to the water's edge.

"I don't feel like swimming," Bertie said. "I don't feel like anything."

"I wish it had been a dog," said Emma.

They sat down. Bertie flipped pebbles into the water. They didn't speak for a while.

"Well, I've got the pictures," Bertie said at last. "If they turn out okay. At least we'll know the village was really there. Why did she smash up the deer?"

Emma shook her head. It was a tangle of dead old roots. She couldn't pull them apart. After that, neither of them mentioned the village directly again, although Emma was sure Bertie was thinking about it just as she was. Instead, they spoke about September and meeting each other back in the city.

Gradually, as they talked about the things they would do together in the far-off autumn, Emma began to feel a kind of hope. She recalled a line from a poem by Emily Dickinson her father had read her. "Hope is the thing with feathers," he had read. She had liked that, not really knowing what it meant. Despite everything, she was beginning to feel rather . . . feathery. The sky was clearing. As the sun emerged, the bay lost its thick look and flashed like small swords at play.

"I loved all those days we had," Bertie said.

"So did I," said Emma with feeling.

"Oh—you don't have to feel so sad," Bertie said. "I've got an uncle who was a shoplifter when he was around fourteen. Well—he didn't pinch big stuff." Suddenly Bertie laughed. "Granny always made him take the stuff back when she found out. The last thing he ever stole, Granny told me, was a big kangaroo doll in a frilly pink dress. The store guard spotted its huge orange feet sticking flat out of my uncle's jacket. My uncle claimed he thought he had picked up his gloves."

"Did he ever get arrested?" Emma asked solemnly.

Bertie grabbed her shoulders and shook her back and forth. "Come on," she demanded, "laugh a little. No, he went to a shrink for a while. Now he's got four kids and he won't let them go to a movie alone. Granny says there's one in every family."

But it wasn't the same, Emma thought.

"I have to go," she said. She smiled at Bertie, who took her hand and pressed it between her own hands.

"I'll see you," Bertie said.

"See you . . ." replied Emma.

~~~~~~~~~~~~~~~~~~

EMMA stood for several minutes on the porch. She hated the thought of finding Uncle Crispin smiling and chatting as if nothing had happened, and Aunt Bea drinking tea. She hated Aunt Bea.

She heard no sound from inside. She walked softly into the foyer, closing the door carefully behind her as she had done that first day.

When she went into the dining room, she saw Uncle Crispin in the kitchen, standing in front of the stove looking down at the burners. Nothing was cooking. He turned and looked at her. "Hello, Emma," he said pensively. As if he'd read her mind, he added, "Bea won't be down this morning. She's not feeling well. She said to say good-bye to you."

Though he spoke quietly, Emma felt as though an iron door had been closed and bolted. She would never know what had gone on in their bedroom when Uncle Crispin returned, without the tea, with the news of Emma's discovery. "Good-bye," that was to be all.

She guessed what would happen when her mother arrived. She would thank Uncle Crispin for taking care of her; she would ask politely after Aunt Bea.

Her mother would be happy not to have to see her. What would it be like? To be a person people were happy not to see?

Suddenly Emma knew that Uncle Crispin would be glad to see her go—not because he didn't like her; she was pretty sure he did—but because he had his wife to take care of. They were all right, the two of them, as long as they were alone. When someone came, Bertie's grandmother, or Emma herself, or anybody at all, it was like ripping open the nest of two creatures in hibernation.

She remembered the hot coal Uncle Crispin had talked about. Was he safe from the heat of it? Burnt to a crispin, she said to herself, thinking he would have liked that joke—at least, part of him would.

She would have been happy now except for that lump of hatred that had lodged in her throat—something she couldn't swallow. Her father had come through the operation; she was going home at any minute.

It happened as she had imagined it would except for one thing. While her mother was putting her things in the back seat of the rented car, Uncle Crispin bent down and said softly in her ear, "I can't say how sorry I am about your sweet village." She couldn't say how sorry she was either. She had not thought of the village as "sweet." She didn't like that description of it; it seemed to make the village less than she knew it to be.

She shook his hand. He was not a person you could throw your arms around and hug. She said thanks for everything—she meant that—and good-bye. And it was over.

Her mother gripped the steering wheel as they drove out from the sandy road, over a bump, to the main road.

"How was it—in a word?" she asked Emma, turning to give her a quick smile.

"Long," replied Emma.

"For me, too," said her mother.

When she had embraced Emma, Emma had felt her rib cage, the sharp bones of her wrists. She had lost weight and she was very pale.

"I'm so relieved to get away from hospital smells," she said. "Walking by those rooms every morning, seeing patients sitting up, looking stunned and weak and scared."

Emma knew her mother was telling her something she wouldn't have told her father. "Daddy's in good shape," she went on. "Although getting completely well takes time. After you've been really sick, you have to think about doing the right thing all the time.

It changes life." She sighed. "I missed you so much. Tell me how it was. What did you do every day? Was it hard with Aunt Bea?"

"Like Daddy said," replied Emma.

"You mean—a terror?" her mother asked.

Emma didn't reply. She had suddenly recalled Aunt Bea crying out that morning that her heart was broken.

"Emma?" her mother questioned. "Well—all those days. I guess a lot happened, too much to tell all at once. I can't help being curious about Bea. I'm sorry she and Daddy aren't close. I always wanted a brother or a sister. But, of course, she was nearly twenty when he was born. It might have been tough even if she wasn't always so—" she hesitated, searching for the right word— "so unhappy. Not that I really know her. . . . I've only seen her a few times over the years."

"But you knew Daddy's mother?"

"Yes, she was a merry, generous woman. Bea made her very glum though, Daddy told me. He said it was as if Bea carried a sign whenever she saw his mother, like someone on strike, saying: *You are an interloper*. And she never once put that sign down."

142

"I met a girl," Emma said, not wanting to think about Aunt Bea for a while. She told her mother how she and Bertie had spent every day on the beach, collecting shells, finding their pictures in the guide to seashore life. She couldn't bring herself to speak of the village yet. To even mention it was to see the torn starfish, the ruined houses, the crushed deer in the yellow circle of the flashlight.

"There are oatmeal cookies in the glove compartment," her mother said.

Emma ate three of them. "I forgot to get any breakfast," she explained.

Her mother reached out her arm and pulled Emma to her side. "It can't have been a picnic," she said. "You didn't complain when I called you up. That was such a help."

Emma felt uneasy. She was concealing not just the misery Aunt Bea had caused her, but the immense pleasure she and Bertie had had in the making of their village.

But Emma was more sleepy than she was uneasy. The heat in the front seat of the car was like warm molasses. She knew she was sinking into it. Her mother said something. "Yes," she said as alertly as she could, not knowing what she was answering. She

143

didn't wake up until her mother shook her gently. The car was idling in front of the apartment house. She was home.

"You go in," her mother said. "Daddy is waiting. I have to park this heap somewhere until I return it to the rental agency."

HE stood with the door wide open. He was wearing a thin, short-sleeved blue shirt and his skin was rosy. He even looked a little plump. Emma walked in and set down her suitcase and shopping bag. She felt a strange shyness, as though she were meeting him for the first time, until he put his arms around her.

"I'm much stronger," he said. "The hospital itself makes a person a little sick but I'm all over that. Put your stuff away. I made you lunch. It's chocolate pudding."

She laughed and he let her go.

"Just chocolate pudding?" she asked.

"Lots of it," he said.

She went to her room. When she woke up tomorrow she would hear city summer sounds outside her window. It would be getting hot pretty soon but she wouldn't mind that too much. She wouldn't ever have to wake up in the silence of the big log house, figuring out how to avoid Aunt Bea.

In the kitchen, she sat down at the small round table where they ate most of their meals unless there was company, when her mother would set up two card tables in the living room for the guests.

Her father had put toasted peanut butter sandwiches in a straw basket. There was a big bowl of chocolate pudding.

"Mom's parking?" he asked, watching her eat.

She nodded. There didn't seem to be a lot to say—not yet anyhow. She wondered what those two were doing now out on Peconic Bay? There would be the steaming teapot, and Uncle Crispin sifting through his music if he had a lesson today. Aunt Bea might lay out a hand of solitaire. Maybe she wouldn't slap the cards down on the table without Emma around. Maybe she wouldn't think so much about all the wrongs that had been done to her without Emma to remind her of all the old ghosts, the big trunk in the closed room upstairs. Would she think about the village? How she had kicked it away?

"You're thinking so hard," her father observed.

"Yes," she said, looking at him, smiling. He didn't ask her what she was thinking about. But she could feel that he was waiting.

145

"Will you get your diary? While we wait for Mom, you can read me what you want to from it."

"I'm sure I didn't write anything except the first day," she said. She couldn't recall what she had written.

"We can start with that," he said. "Then you can just tell me."

She got up and went to her room and took the diary from the bag. There was so little in it, it was easy to find what she'd written.

I'm here, it said. *Uncle Crispin is really nice. The bay and the beach are great. Aunt Bea is—*

Something had been added where she had left off. It wasn't in her handwriting. The letters were big and plump and round. *"Aunt Bea is—"* she read aloud, *"a sad bad old woman."*

She put down the diary on the table. Only a few hours ago, when Emma had gone downstairs in the big log house, she remembered she had heard the sound of those white moccasins whispering across the floor. Aunt Bea had gone into her room, had written those words about herself in the diary.

The lump she had felt inside ever since she had told herself she hated Aunt Bea dissolved all at once. She breathed deeply. It felt like the first real breath she had taken in days; it was like what her father had described to her, "drawing up a pail of fresh cold water from a well."

Aunt Bea *would* have looked in her diary. It was just like her. But what she had written for Emma to see was not like her, not as Emma had known her. It wasn't an apology. It was, Emma felt, something deeper, a secret about herself.

She would keep it a secret, Emma knew, all of it. She picked up the diary. It was as though she was holding Aunt Bea in her hand, and she had grown as light as the piece of balsa wood Bertie had found that said: *Lodgings*. She took the diary and put it on a shelf in her closet.

When she walked back into the kitchen, her father smiled up at her expectantly.

"I hardly wrote a word," she said. "But I'll tell you about it."

She sat down. "We built a village, my friend Bertie and I," she began.